LIVING CINEMA

LIVING CINEMA

New Directions in Contemporary Film-making

Louis Marcorelles

with the collaboration of Nicole Rouzet-Albagli

Translated by Isabel Quigly

PRAEGER PUBLISHERS

New York · Washington

BOOKS THAT MATTER

Published in the United States of America in 1973
by Praeger Publishers, Inc.,
111 Fourth Avenue, New York, N.Y. 10003

Translated from the French
Eléments pour un nouveau cinéma
© Unesco 1970

This translation © George Allen & Unwin Ltd, 1973

Library of Congress Catalog Card Number: 79–186476

Printed in Great Britain

FOREWORD

This book was undertaken at the suggestion of the cultural division of Unesco to give an account of a group of meetings they sponsored that dealt with new techniques of communication. The most important of these were held in Florence, Mannheim and Budapest.

The report we had envisaged very soon became, with the agreement of those involved in it, a personal, documented analysis of the problems raised by these new techniques and of the people using them. The distinction made in the book between the two main currents is not really satisfactory. The part dealing with 'direct cinema' does seem to provide a solid basis for possible study in the future, but the short section entitled 'concrete cinema' merely suggests ideas for further study. However if, for the first time, we are looking at what is happening in 'new cinema' throughout the world, then it is necessary to deal with this side of it.

Nearly all the original book has been preserved in the English edition, with a few small corrections and an important addition, giving further information, to the chapter on Pierre Perrault. A new postscript at the end, 'Into the Seventies', makes a modest attempt to put 'direct cinema' into the context of work done by Jean-Luc Godard and Jean-Marie Straub, where documentary and fiction merge.

Madame Nicole Rouzet-Albagli, teacher of philosophy, wrote two chapters and I suggested them: 'The Small Screen' and 'Technique as Work'. My thanks to Ann Head, of *The Observer*, for checking through the book, and to Isabel Quigly for her excellent translation.

L.M.

CONTENTS

ART CENTER COLLEGE OF DESIGN

ILLUSTRATIONS

Introduction

From 2 to 5 March 1963 the MIPE-TV (*Marché international des programmes et équipements de télévision*) held a working conference at Lyons. This event might be considered the departure point for a realisation of the importance of light-weight equipment in attempting to capture reality in the most accurate way, and for an understanding of the technical problems involved. In September 1968 the last of these Unesco meetings was held in Montreal and its programme sums up what had been happening during the five years between the two meetings: 'Conference on the cultural value of the cinema, radio and television in contemporary society.'

A meeting of film people has rarely been as pleasant, as open and as effective as the working conference at Lyons, which was arranged with the collaboration of Pierre Schaeffer and his research team at the ORTF. Professionals met – among them people who had worked with portable camera units, such as Leacock, Maysles, Pennebaker and Brault, French *cinéma-vérité* directors like Rouch and Ruspoli, and a pioneer of cinema in the street, Morris Engel. In all they said the memory of neo-realism was constantly present.

America, the promised land of a cinema without limitations, was discovered. At first, it looked as if these discussions would give way to real changes in the use of the camera, but unfortunately only sociologists, psychologists and officially approved theorists were from then on to speak on the subject. Speculation took the place of concrete examples, and it became clear that there was no ideological framework for the idea of 'direct cinema'. This meant that the revolutionary contribution of this new cinema was neglected, although we must not forget another kind of cinema – 'concrete cinema' – to which we shall return briefly in a later section.

The danger, which was never avoided, was that people

would talk about the cinema from the outside. Most irritating of all is to find a man as distinguished as Marshall McLuhan, the mouthpiece of the electronic age, talking about television without even mentioning the cinema, or contrasting the two in the sketchiest way; or to see Christian Metz who, with Jean Mitry, is the most serious living theorist on the structure of the cinema, restricting his field of investigation at the very beginning, and to all intents and purposes sticking to the kind of cinema in which the image is all-important, in the tradition of the work, both theoretical and practical, of the great Russians, and of Bela Balasz.

Marshall McLuhan contrasts the electronic age with the mechanical age, and prefers the tactile to the once dominant linear and visual qualities. He distinguishes between the 'hot' medium and the 'cool' medium, in other words between television and the cinema, television presupposing the intense participation of a group that can move freely about a room or some other place that is more or less illuminated, while the cinema depends on the fascination and magic of moving images and sound emanating from a high screen on to a passive audience. This seems to us quite indefensible. It is not enough to say, as a corollary, that Bergman or Fellini have made the audience participate much more actively, and that the audience, although at one time passive, has suddenly begun to use its mind. It might be better to bear the spirit of the following in mind:

1. The Hollywood cinema, which is quite clearly the model for McLuhan's ideas, is today a fringe cinema, a pure object of consumption; in the future one can imagine it being computerised with a suitable programme.

2. Bergman and Fellini, if we forget all aesthetic considerations, are the post-war equivalents of Pagnol and Carné, perpetuating a cinema that is theatrical or essentially plastic, on the fringes of the Hollywood industry (relatively speaking), but already extremely old-fashioned as well.

3. Direct cinema, with which we shall be dealing at length later on and which will form the core of this book, means an abrupt break with the present ways of filming and acting –

12

the only ones recognised at the moment. We are coming to a new, hybrid art, which is not exactly cinema in the traditional sense nor entirely television in the commercial American sense.

'Direct cinema' is inspired by a rigorous discipline, a discipline in which man, the creator, still predominates; but he is creator in a very different way from directors like Fellini, Antonioni, Resnais, and so on. It is not a question of knowing whether the medium is, or is not, the message, or whether the mould in which our modern lives flow irrevocably imprisons them, for better or worse. McLuhan ought, perhaps, to have known rather more about the cinema, to have realised that two things were happening in it: on the one hand, 'new cinemas' were springing up all over the world and, on the other, a 'new cinema' was being worked out, in the aesthetic and historical meaning of the words. This is what we shall be dealing with in future chapters. How regrettable that a man as distinguished as McLuhan should have so elementary a view of the cinema! Other writers may not admit as frankly as Roland Barthes does that the cinema is something completely foreign to them; but many of them react to it in a way that is not fundamentally different from that of their parents and grandparents. Wittgenstein is said to have sat in the front row of dark cinemas in order to lose himself in the screen and 'empty' his spirit.

Christian Metz, Roland Barthes' follower and author of a series of careful *Essais sur la signification au cinéma* (Editions Klincksieck, 1968), cannot be accused of such an attitude. For the first time since Jean Mitry, perhaps, a systematic study has been made of the processes that make up a film, in the light of structuralism. This is not the place to examine his work in detail. It would appear to have only one fault, but that a very serious one: it immobilises the film, shows it as flat, romantically continuous, and dominated by the visual; sound, and particularly sound as it is used in direct cinema, is really not considered. For Drew and Leacock's *Football*, a film that is certainly not flawless but implies a great deal, Metz has nothing but sarcasm. All he sees in it is crazy zooms, and he makes no effort to understand the mechanics that went into this style of film-making, or the directors' wish to take a fuller part in the

13

making of the film. All he says is things like: 'He (the maker of direct cinema films) too often gives up the illusions of art.' Tied as he is to the ideas of the 'classic' cinema, Metz does not even try to analyse logically the process of creation and perception in the direct cinema we shall be dealing with later.

Metz is also limited by his lack of knowledge of what is called experimental cinema, whether it is the 'underground' cinema of the United States, in its many forms, or the work of Pierre Schaeffer and his research team in Paris. He describes the experimental cinema as being 'cascades of gratuitous, anarchical images against a background of noise, decorated with words that are inflated and supposedly advanced' (this last is presumably aimed at Schaeffer's group). Later he says peremptorily: '. . . even where there is artistry involved, each fragment is not used with art'. Has he no knowledge of Norman McLaren's many films in Canada, or those of Stan Brakhage in the United States, in which the film is used in the same way that the painter uses his canvas, the sculptor his marble, and the chemist his solutions? You cannot talk about the cinema without first going humbly back to its technical beginnings, to creation in the strictest, most craftsmanly meaning of the word.

Finally, I found no serious mention of television in *Essais sur la signification au cinéma.* Of course, Christian Metz has logic on his side. The spoken word, in the sense that he knows nothing about, is something quite new in the cinema; it is not something static and immobile, taken from books, but something 'living' (as with Richard Leacock), or 'lived' (as with with Pierre Perrault), and it has acquired a new life since the advent of television. There is no point in trying to connect it with a completely old-fashioned idea of cinema, nor in deceptively proclaiming the importance of the verbal, even 'literary', element in Alain Resnais, Chris Marker or Agnès Varda.[1]

At one of the linguistic seminars at the New Cinema Festival in Pesaro, I reproached Christian Metz with all this, and he answered with disarming candour: 'But you've got to begin at the beginning. I haven't got past 1929!' This is really 'la recherche du cinéma perdu'! Metz takes so narrow a view that he

[1]See Christian Metz, *Essais sur la signification au cinéma,* p. 62, 'The text becomes the image, the image becomes the text . . .'

deliberately avoids facing the basic changes which have taken place in the cinema since the advent of the spoken word and particularly since the advent of 'direct cinema', a type of cinema established by television and Leacock's first films in 1961 (*Yanqui No!* and *Primary*). Occasionally he does stress the importance of speech, but only so as to see it used in a static, literary way.

But for the first time in history speech can move, breathe, be seen, take up space. At the other extreme, in some of the underground films, the image is the only thing that matters: it has no narrative meaning and becomes pure material, sometimes an empty canvas, or a block of stone or marble, sometimes a note and a vibration; this is the truly 'senseless' cinema. The extremes meet: on the one hand, Leacock tries to use pure forms (a fragment inserted into a performance of Alban Berg's opera *Lulu* in Brooklyn in 1967); and, on the other, Andy Warhol with his voracious camera, literally 'jokes' with synchronised sound in *Chelsea Girls* (1966).

The cinema must be considered, and reconsidered, from within, through its own structure, and not as some bizarre mixture of sound and image in which the silent film and the written, literary word are oddly mingled.

The Birth of Young Cinemas

Young cinema is today established all over the world and should not be oversimplified. The great directors of the silent Soviet cinema, working parallel with the political and artistic excitement of the USSR, were not yet out of the twenties when they hurled themselves euphorically into the maddest experiments. Those pillars of Hollywood, John Ford, King Vidor and Raoul Walsh, conquered both the West and the cinema with their youthful enthusiasm. René Clair and Jean Renoir also began when they were very young. Today's problems are quite different.

The American, Soviet and French film-makers were not concerned with 'fighting', at one and the same time, both the cinema and their own country. The communist revolution had been established once and for all, free enterprise reigned by divine right in America, and the French *avant-garde* was not trying to knock anything down except the temple of conformity. It needed the shock of the Second World War, and then the coming of television during the fifties (1949 in the United States), to alter the situation radically. It was Italian neo-realism, under the leadership of Zavattini, De Sica and Rossellini, that first upset the idea of performance and dramatic continuity based on nicely calculated effects. This had reached perfection of a kind in the thirties in Hollywood – otherwise known as 'the dream-factory' – after the coming of the talkies.

The camera went out into the streets, and non-professional actors played ordinary people, without special effects or elaborate lighting. As the post-war years receded the Italian cinema gradually lost its force and was carried away by its own economic miracle to become, today, a kind of European branch of Hollywood; yet its early example was not wasted or lost, either in Europe or in Latin America. Film-makers agreed to work on shoestring budgets, ignore the old rules of

16

action and narrative; they would linger over some piece of décor, waste time, speak frankly about things not mentioned in polite society . . . Milos Forman, in an interview, explained how he and his young fellow-students at FAMU, the Prague film school, welcomed these Italian films in which anything could be said, and which were shown in Czechoslovakia at the time of the 'cult of personality'. They were shown as examples of Western bourgeois decadence, but to Forman and his friends they seemed a call to free criticism. Why, they wondered, shouldn't they try to get the freedom in films that Italy had in 1945 and 1946?

The French 'New Wave', which at the beginning was strongly influenced by Italy's example – and this applied particularly to François Truffaut – was to prove an even more decisive upheaval. When, in November 1958, Truffaut made his first full-length film, he kept to the neo-realist example of poverty, film-making on a shoestring, and free expression. The great difference between the young French film-makers and the Italians before them was that the young French directors were much less critical of the society they lived in, and did not reject it outright. They wanted, more than anything, to make films, and cared little how they managed it. They – or at least the *Cahiers du Cinéma* group – refused to subscribe to the myths about technique or to the left-wing attitudes that were then rampant. Another group, sometimes known as the 'left bank' group (Resnais, Varda, Marker, Colpi), tended to make cinema either a substitute or a mere platform for literature. Truffaut and his colleagues made film confessions, very much like first novels, whereas the films of the 'left bank' group clearly had more 'distinguished' literary models: the *nouveau roman*, Giraudoux, Marguerite Duras. Alain Resnais was heir to the French classic cinema, that of Carné and Clément, but it was François Truffaut who conveyed the tone of France to those outside it and who became the symbol of radical revolt against the prevailing structure in the cinema.

He stood up to the established production system, proved that it was possible to work with very small teams of technicians and to come across on the screen directly and personally (for instance, in *Les Quatre Cents Coups*, a film that was partly autobiographical). A year later, Godard made his own attempt at wrecking the whole system outright (*A Bout de Souffle*). It does not matter that Truffaut is now part of the newly-established system that took over from the earlier one (he makes low-budget films for the Americans, who seem to have lost the secret of it); it does not matter that he has never clearly denounced society as it stands today. His example has been followed in Rio de Janeiro, in Montreal and in Budapest, that is, in an underdeveloped capitalist country, an overdeveloped capitalist country and a socialist country, with the necessary modifications. Before he made films himself Truffaut was a virulent film critic, denouncing French methods and praising what was dynamic in Hollywood; he also had the advantage that he was the first film-maker to speak for the postwar generation. A visit to Rio or Montreal in 1962 would have shown what Truffaut and Godard meant to the young rebels filled with a passionate love for the cinema, who wanted to turn it into a weapon that could be used against what they saw as a flagrantly unjust society.

This is where we can really begin to speak of 'young cinema'; because at the festivals and among film enthusiasts 'young cinema' was soon to mean the cinema of either the Third World, of countries without a film history at all, or of countries alienated from the dominant film industries – the United States in the first place, then France, Italy and Germany among the capitalist countries, and the USSR among the socialist countries. People began to free themselves from the paralysing influence of these models, and to try to create original, national cinemas, which allowed them to discover their own national identity.

Around 1964 two film-makers have symbolised this desire to liberate the cinema of their own country: Glauber Rocha with *Black God, White Devil* in Brazil, and Gilles Groulx with *Le Chat dans le Sac* in French Canada. Both acknowledged the problem in the decisive March 1966 issue of *Cahiers du Cinéma*. First, Glauber Rocha:

'We think that the cinema may be a powerful instrument in promoting knowledge of what Brazil is really like, that it may challenge this reality, that it may even have an overwhelming influence. It may become an instrument of political agitation.

18

The Brazilian cinema has started from this single principle,
which allows all kinds of things to be done according to each
director's temperament. The expression *cinema nôvo* (the
name given to the films of Glauber Rocha and his friends)
means that our cinema has only just been born. What existed
before was merely craftsmanship, without any cultural or
industrial meaning. Today *cinema nôvo* is the Brazilian
cinema, and its history is being written in the same way as
the most important chapters in Brazil's history are being
written . . . A cinema that intends not to be alienated must
obviously prove that it has avoided becoming academic.
Brazil's cultural tradition is extremely complex and so it
allows a great variety of styles to its film-makers, although
they have a common basis. To court the public by making
traditionalist or formalist films would be to deny the very
existence of our movement. If we have not yet reached the
public as much as we would wish, it is because we have not
yet found the right way in which to overcome myths and
alienation. That is what we are trying to do.'

Less exalted and more secretive, Gilles Groulx, citizen of the
province of Quebec, writing at a time when the prospects were
much bleaker for the French Canadians, said simply:

'When we try to find what the problems of our culture mean,
we become aware that our uneasiness is not artistic but social:
we might call it an attempt to express the man born in this
country . . . When I look at cinema, I do not wonder whether
what we show is true or illusory compared with some truth
in itself. To me, creation in the cinema is essentially subjective
and determined by the "lived".'

In the same number of *Cahiers* there appears this disturbing
passage, which may explain the deep fighting spirit that has to
sustain all 'young cinema' in post-colonial or partly-colonial
countries, also from a French Canadian:

'Our contacts with Europe, as you know, were few. Somewhere in Europe, someone had probably decided that everything that belonged to America must be American, which

19

meant more or less English. Europe does not like accidents. Here we keep quiet, living enigmatically, without prestige . . . Dependence being a fact, the idea of liberation seems right. As the cinema is an expression of culture, we think that it will be an instrument of liberation.'

Six years after the beginning of the New Wave, Glauber Rocha's *Black God. White Devil* and Gilles Groulx's *Le Chat dans le Sac* have become landmarks in the history of new cinema. They were in a sense far more influential than *Les Quatre Cents Coups* or *A Bout de Souffle*, and proved that a definite change was taking place all over the world. An uneasy balance is being established between political and film necessity. Sometimes there have been clashes with the established authorities. The welcome artistic minorities in their own countries have given them proves that Groulx and Rocha were right in their aims. But here comparison between them stops. In the next chapter we shall return at greater length to the originality of the French-Canadian cinema; today, it has become a leading force in world cinema, and, like *cinema nôvo*, it is engaged in a hard struggle.

Less original, and with fewer outlets, is the Hungarian cinema. In a socialist country no change of policy, and therefore of artistic policy, can ever come about haphazardly. The Hungarian cinema is tied to tradition much more than the other two are, but it has incomparably better technical resources than the Brazilians, for instance. In 1965, a young filmmaker aged twenty-seven, Istvan Szabo, managed to break out of the strait-jacket and make his first film, *The Age of Daydreams*, using his own script and techniques that were closer to those of the New Wave than to the old academic ideas of central Europe. The French influence on his film is obvious, yet the tone remains original because of its historical context. For the first time the tragedy of 1956 was dealt with fairly frankly. In the film six youngsters make a vow, when they finish their studies, that they will never part; but life and work, illness and death soon divide them. Szabo ostensibly pays tribute to Truffaut in his film, although, as a beginner, he never tries to go beyond the new conventions Truffaut established. What matters, though, is that the young people on the screen

20

are really alive, that the camera gets out into the street, that their childhood, when they shared the excitement of seeing socialism on the march, is still close to them in 1956; all this meant a breakthrough in the rigid, well-made Hungarian cinema of the time.

One could go on forever describing the chain reaction which films like this are producing all over the world. There are no strict rules about it. The Swiss Romands may feel certain affinities with the French Canadians of Quebec, since both are reacting against an extremely rich consumer society; but there are great differences between them. Both are linguistic minorities, but the Swiss Romands are masters of their own particular environment whereas the French Canadians are subordinate to a strongly centralised power. Differences in the way French was spoken in Canada and in France for a long time seemed an insurmountable obstacle between the two countries, just as an Australian or New Zealand accent seems bewildering to someone from London or New York.

In the Third World, the idea of 'young cinema' can really expand. An example of a country now forging a tool that is completely its own is Senegal. Led by one of the strongest personalities in the cinema today, Ousmane Sembène, an autonomous black African cinema is slowly being born, with its own troubles and trials, yet knowing quite well that it has an audience ready to support it. Sembène was once a docker, then a writer, and he made up his mind to speak directly to his fellow countrymen. He studied in Moscow under Mark Donskoi, and also worked with French technicians and in French laboratories. He is a long way from the excitement of *cinema nôvo*, or the jansenism of *Le Chat dans le Sac*. He likes to tell his story in a very classical way, making slowly but surely for its object. But for the first time an African language – Ouolof, spoken by the majority of the Senegalese people – was heard on the screen in his feature film, *The Mandate*.

The problem, in Rio, in Montreal, or in Dakar (it is slightly different in Budapest), is to find places where these films may be shown, since foreign films – American, French and Italian – monopolise the screens. One would hope that the government of the country concerned might give practical support to an independent cinema. The wonderful thing about these young

21

cinemas, all struggling desperately for recognition from their own people, is that they are found, not in one or two countries, or even in five or six, but in ten, fifteen or twenty. And success spreads. How far can these young cinemas communicate freely among themselves? How far will their films be shown independently, unburdened by the payment of heavy dues? How will they be received in our old, blasé countries, with their ideas of the consumer society and their out-worn values? Both here and in the country of origin Unesco should give invaluable help by passing round information and arranging exchanges. The day every original film, however different from our Western idea of an original film, has the right to be shown in east, west, north and south, should be hastened in every way possible.

Even supposing this could be done, there would still be a fundamental necessity. Once 'young' cinemas have become established throughout the world, how can they in turn become qualitatively 'new'? How can they take the step from reform to revolution? At present it is impossible to foresee what the Third World, or small nations until now unable to speak through the cinema, will produce. Judging by what exists at the moment, there would seem to be two main currents with which a new cinema is likely to flow. On the one hand there is 'direct cinema', which, by using portable cameras, immediately becomes part of living reality, and on the other there is 'concrete cinema', created entirely (or almost entirely) by the hand of man, working on the image itself, often image by image. A kind of sur-realism has, as its perfectly symmetrical corollary, irrealism or non-realism. Naturalism, that dangerous terrain, is something we have really moved beyond.

DIRECT CINEMA

Direct Cinema

'*This is not the script from which* Don't look Back *was made. The film was made without a script. This is simply a transcript of what happened and what was said. It is as accurate as the fallible human ear can make it. It is no substitute for the reality of the film. Since that sense (of reality) is missing (it explains itself in the film), it is necessary to tell something of the conditions under which the film was made.*

'*A sort of complicated game. Neither side quite knows the rules. The cameraman (myself) can only film what happens. There are no retakes. I never attempted to direct or control the action. People said whatever they wanted and did whatever. The choice of action lay always with the person being filmed. Naturally, I edited the material as I believed it should appear, but with the absolute conviction that any attempt to distort events or remarks would somehow reveal itself and subject the whole to suspicion. The order of the film is almost entirely chronological and nothing was staged or arranged for the purpose of the film. It is not my intention to extol or denounce or even explain Dylan, or any of the characters therein. This is only a kind of record of what happened.*'

D. A. Pennebaker's introduction to the book of his film *Don't Look Back* (Ballantine Books, 1968).

'*I think that, without the cinema, you couldn't get to meet people as varied as those I've met. Because you've got no reason to talk to them, to ask them questions, to get inside them. When you listen to someone talking for ten minutes, you hear a certain number of things. If you've taped what he said and play it back the next day, you hear ten times as much. This is particularly so when you're talking to ordinary people, and there are all sorts of words you don't follow at once because of accents and intonations and because they're talking fast: but if you've got it down on tape you can listen to it slowly until you know it, reproduce it, assimilate it. How can I put it? Alexis[1] is dead, and yet he talks to me again. Does that mean he's still alive? Now, there's a mystery. Because as he wasn't an actor, as he wasn't someone playing someone else, it's really he who's there in the words I'm listening to. Of course he's there in his image as well, but I don't need his image to see him! Sometimes I think there's no other man in the world who's left as many words as Alexis. It is extraordinary, of course, but it is the meaning of this phenomenon that is important. You know, people have been talking since the world began. They talked before they wrote, but all we know about the people who talked is what was written down, and here suddenly you can possess their words just as they are, and examine them. And in fifty years people will be able to examine words that have been spoken today. This is especially important, I think, for ordinary people, who have always been translated by people unlike themselves, that is, novelists and dramatists, like Molière, who translated the language of servants. But it's not the servant expressing himself directly. And I think that today, thanks to the cinema and tape recording, we're going to think differently about things and in particular about man, simple man, who has never expressed himself.*'

Pierre Perrault speaking to J.-L. Comolli and André Labarthe in the television programme 'Pierre Perrault ou l'action parlée'.

[1]Alexis played the main part in Pierre Perrault's films *Pour la Suite du Monde* (made in 1963, in collaboration with Michel Brault) and *Le Règne du Jour* (1967). These will be dealt with at length in the chapter on the French-Canadian cinema.

From the very beginning of the cinema, efforts were made to synchronise sound and image, by making a camera and a gramophone function simultaneously; but the early films were so soon successful that research was not taken any further. It needed the spur of a financial crisis in Hollywood for the talking cinema to be tackled energetically, and it has existed, broadly speaking, since 1929. In the United States and in France, synchronisation seemed just a necessary part of commercial production. But what sort of synchronisation was it?

Once the first amazement was over, the mere fact that lips moved in time to words, thus strengthening the impression of reality, had no particular artistic merit. Most synchronised commercial films are made in the studio, just as they were when the talkies began. The cameras may be more mobile, but they are still not very much so; they have a few stock movements – either very simple ones, or else very complicated ones. The camera is radically outside the event being filmed; it is a kind of god, sitting in judgement. The lighting effects, the choice of angles for takes and, later on at the cutting stage, efforts to achieve a particular rhythm: all these hark back to the beginning of the silent cinema, when what really mattered was the image. The sound is merely an addition, it verifies the fact that the action shown on the screen is in fact being lived through by people with the gift of speech. And this speech technicians never cease trying to make as audible and as smooth as it is possible for it to be.

Professional script-writers write dialogue that has no surprises in it, and aims to be understood as clearly as possible by the audience. Even when the film can be considered an art form, as in the case of Resnais and other rather literary directors, the only object of having a script, either taken from some earlier work or else written specially for the screen, seems to be to sustain a subtle, varied story and a flowing, personal prose which in turn will support images, the whole object of which is to illustrate what is written, what has somehow been pre-established.

The heavy literary heritage that has weighed for so long on the cinema is shown in a whole battery of stylistic figures – metaphors, symbols, ellipses. There is an excellent little book

27

on the subject, thought by Truffaut to be a model of its kind –
François Chevassu's *Le Langage cinématographique*. The
desire to codify a 'film language', starting from a group of
fundamental rules, makes one think that a film has got to be
made according to technical rules on cutting, direction and
montage, rules established in the very early days of cinema.
Sheer laziness!

The Technique of Direct Cinema[1]

The equipment used by the film-maker specialising in direct
cinema is lighter than that of the traditional cinema. However,
if he is seeking perfection it is also fairly expensive. Without
going into any detailed scientific analysis of the various instruments used, we will sum up some of the objectives of those
using portable camera units. The most important object is to
prevent the recording of images and sounds from being a slave
to technique, and to make the equipment used extremely
mobile.

The silent camera – of the Arriflex, Auricon, Coutant, or
Debrie kind – weighs around twenty pounds, which means
that it is not easy for the amateur to handle unless he is pretty
strong. Albert Maysles likes to balance his camera comfortably
on his shoulder, so that its weight is divided – half in front and
half behind – and so that it allows a man to take up a comfortable position while he is filming. Americans like Leacock and
Pennebaker, who like filming 'off the hip', as they put it, which
means that the camera is held against the body without any
solid support or control apart from muscular strength, take a
kind of 'physical' film-making as far as it will go, and their
participation in what is happening gives an unequalled sense

[1] On this subject the following are of interest: Mario Ruspoli's
Le Groupe synchrone léger, written for Unesco in 1963 and still the best
introduction to direct cinema; and interviews with Robert Drew and
Richard Leacock (*Cahiers du Cinéma*, February 1963), and with Jean
Rouch (*Cahiers du Cinéma*, June 1963) where the film-maker's need to
free himself from the paralysing restrictions involved in the use of heavy
equipment is shown even more clearly. The kind of equipment used in
direct cinema can easily be carried by two people, a cameraman and a
sound recorder. The sound recorder is usually a small person and can
move about unnoticed; later he helps with the cutting.

of their particular presence in their best films. Lighter cameras, weighing three or four kilos, like the Coutant prototype which Jean Rouch and Michel Brault used in making *Chronique d'un Été*, and Mario Ruspoli and Michel Brault used in *Les Inconnus de la Terre*, have appeared on the market. This does not matter much. Indeed, the very weight of the camera may help to link a film-maker with the actual weight of the things he is filming.

Sound and image may be synchronised by processes Mario Ruspoli has described as wires linking the camera to the recorder. The wire guarantees a reproduction of what has been caught on the microphone that is more or less accurate and has no surprises about it. But it may annoy the cameraman who, if he wants to involve himself closely in the action, has to move about among people. Today, the people to be filmed can behave as they like, because they do not have to be in contact with any wires. Fast filming means that the minimum of lighting can be used, or no additional lighting at all. Directional microphones help to localise the recording of sound in open spaces, to restrict the area in which sound may usefully be taken.

Working on sound, which is infinitely more delicate than working on the image, demands instruments that have achieved a fine degree of precision and sensitivity. Here I agree entirely with Marshall McLuhan in welcoming the advent of sound and of the living word in a world until now ruled entirely by the written word. But only a man who knows how to carry and use a microphone can get anything out of it. Stefan Kudeslki, inventor of the famous Nagra portable tape recorders, says that he can take down *everything* transmitted to him through the microphone. Such tape recorders are now used in Hollywood for classic film-making, because they record sound more faithfully than any other instruments used in the past.

An almost plastic use of sound can already be envisaged. The difficulty is to keep the main sound uncluttered by secondary sounds, and yet preserve the rich amount of sound which the normally formed ear is able to take in. Although excellent results have been achieved by the use of straightforward, recited speech, without interference, serious problems still face the film-maker using fully fledged, integral direct cinema.

Most people filmed with direct synchronised sound are given a so-called Lavalier microphone which hangs round the neck. The Americans, though, would rather use one held on the end of a rod, the sound man having to follow the action discreetly and tirelessly. Richard Leacock thinks that the recording of sound is an art. For instance, he said how glad he was to have once worked with a young German acting student who managed to play with the phonetic interpretation of sound and, through it, the dramatic interpretation of the words that had just been spoken.

One final, essential point: it is possible to make 35 mm films in the spirit of direct cinema, that is by seeking to reveal thoughts and actions through an underlying layer of words. Original works have been made in this way, but without the camera being able to move away from certain pre-established points. The film-maker's intellectual liveliness then has to compensate for his static equipment. There are 35 mm cameras which are as light as the 16 mm ones we mentioned, or even lighter, but they have the disadvantage of being much too noisy.

Direct cinema has a meaning only if it uses 16 mm films (which are becoming progressively easier to blow up to 35 mm later on). One could describe 16 mm as not so much a technique as a state of mind, the natural breathing of an art that has been revived through contact with the real world. With it, the cinema and its history may begin all over again.

The Aesthetic of Direct Cinema[1]

A technical revolution almost immediately leads to aesthetic problems and to the need for a corresponding revolution in aesthetics. Although I disagree profoundly with Christian Metz in his way of seeing, hearing and thinking – in the best sense of the word – about the cinema, I admit that, in *Le Cinéma moderne et la narrativité*, he dared to deny that a 'grammar' of film can be imposed upon film-making, as a number of experts would like it to be. In the cinema there are

[1] This section, like other parts of the book, finds its inspiration in Louis Marcorelles' *Une Esthétique du réel, le cinéma direct* published by Unesco in 1963.

no rules of correct behaviour, there is no Academy to lay down the law.

This being the case, anything goes. You do not have to film from this angle or from that. As there has been a technical revolution, let us try to formulate tentatively an aesthetic of direct cinema, of the creation of the beautiful with the informal and the non-organised. In the December 1963 – January 1964 special American number of *Cahiers du Cinéma* Jean-Luc Godard shot a number of poisoned arrows at Richard Leacock, although he was quite prepared to graze in his pastures. What he said was full of inaccuracies although lively and superficially sharp. It exposed the real breach between concepts of the cinema as about antagonistic as it is possible to be:

'Across the Atlantic, *cinéma-vérité* is translated as "candid camera". And candid Leacock certainly is, in more ways than one, chasing about after truth without even wondering on which side of the Pyrenees his objective is to be found. What truth is it all about, then? By failing to separate cause and effect, by mixing the rule and the exception, Leacock and his team do not realise that what their eye is enclosing in the camera's sights is both more and less than the recording instrument the camera uses . . . yet never merely this instrument, which may remain a recording instrument or may become a fountain pen or a paint brush. Deprived of awareness in this way, Leacock's camera, in spite of its honesty, loses the two fundamental qualitities of a camera: intelligence and sensitivity. It is no use having a clear image if one's intentions are muddled.'

There is plenty of nonsense here: inaccurate references to *cinéma vérité*, a branch of direct cinema that we shall be looking at later, and to the 'candid camera', invented by the English-speaking Canadians on the basis of what Cartier-Bresson had experienced and sought: in other words, an art that was basically photographic in conception, little influenced by the idea of using sound. The flaws in Godard's argument show clearly through: if he had the experience needed to hold a 16 mm synchronised camera like Leacock, Pennebaker or Maysles, he would find himself forced to make other choices, and not to

31

rely only on mere systematic provocation. He would have to read, to dig into the way things go and the life of beings 'as they really are', as Brecht put it. An entire moral attitude is involved, one that demands communication between the film-maker and the people filmed. What matters is no longer some piece of fiction that emerges, full-grown and finished, from the mind of an individual film-maker. Cutting no longer consists in short-circuiting irresponsibly filmed material according to some subjective whim, but in integrating a deeply subjective personal perception of life with the objective reality of what is seen.

The danger of Leacock's attitude – it is the only one Godard considers – is that when the film-maker and his audience participate too strongly *in* what is happening, the sense of reality, its deepest significance, is lost. But, on the other hand, we have never been so deeply involved in this reality. The intensity of our feeling is the sign of a new quality in perception and it is up to us to draw from it whatever consequences we may. Direct cinema, at its highest, looks at life with a kind of dual passion: through shooting and editing, indissolubly linked. Godard, in films like *La Chinoise* and *Weekend* (made, admittedly, a long time after these statements of his, so that he may have changed his mind since then), does not go deeply into the problems of pro-Chinese young people or the bourgeoisie as victims of the consumer society, but shows us his own obsessions, his own inhibitions and his own tireless curiosity. In Leacock's case, on the contrary, if his particular eye were not irreplaceable, the least important thing about a Leacock film would be Leacock himself. Pierre Perrault enters into his own films rather more actively, and does not actually hold the camera himself, yet the movement of his films is a regular one: coming-and-going, systole-diastole, characters-Perrault-characters. This movement enriches what he shows as much as it is possible to do, revealing his characters without making them do a strip-tease; whereas Godard, however sincere he may have been in some of his most recent films, merely carries on the ideas of the traditional cinema, although he puts them into a modern idiom. In his blatant way he uses direct cinema only as a trick, never attempting any deeper, intenser understanding of things as they really are.

32

The two long quotations at the beginning of this section from D. A. Pennebaker, who has always been Leacock's colleague and *alter ego*, and from Pierre Perrault, contain all the elements for a basic criticism of direct cinema, both as a form in itself and as a form of cinema to be compared with old-style film-making; and they point out, in opposite ways, the two main routes which direct cinema is bound to take.

Pierre Perrault's *Le Règne du Jour* and D. A. Pennebaker's *Don't Look Back* also appeared in book form. I myself have seen them both, listening very carefully to the dialogues, working hard to transcribe what Leacock and Pennebaker call the 'living' word, and Perrault calls the 'lived' word. Pennebaker says definitely, and Perrault does not deny, that 'it is as precise as the fallible human ear can be'. But here the resemblance between the two men ends. The pragmatic Pennebaker believes in raw reporting: things exist, let us express them as they have never been expressed before. The French-Canadian Perrault, who was once a writer – poet, playwright, user of language – finds another way of making contact with people: the 'objectivised' word (perhaps in opposition to Leacock's word 'objectivising'). It is not mere chance that Perrault's films are above all a reconstruction of the past through the present, that they start from a 'conservationist' historical plan, with every kind of imaginable subtlety; whereas Leacock and Pennebaker care only about reality on the move, heightened, indeed overcharged, with meaning.

With Perrault, Leacock and Pennebaker, whatever their differences, the people they seek to show objectively are no less dramatically exciting than the characters in the most fantastic fictional stories of the traditional cinema. The audience has to be intensely involved, and there are none of the traditional tricks of the trade to help this involvement along. The camera is nearly always at the height of a man, the lighting is haphazard, the director cannot prettify what he sees or use what is not strictly necessary. The sound – the totality of sound – sets the tone of what is happening. In the classical cinema, even with synchronised sound, the action is all drawing-room action with everything bright and shiny, antiseptic, and nearly always false. Our advanced film-makers have made the alterations in style

c

that are needed in using 35 mm cameras, yet they refuse to be really radical, to go back to square one and make films without preconceived ideas and with really malleable performances. The changes that are needed have nothing to do with the vague, nameless expressionism they have inherited from the silent cinema.

The actors, whether professional or not, would become totally involved in their roles, and in a way they would become fellow-creators of the film. This might begin to answer the demands of Bertolt Brecht.

Obviously direct cinema has a great deal to do with the development of television, although it is not, in itself, really television. The limitations and opaqueness of the small screen mean that images must be composed in a particular way, that the close-ups become all-important. Besides, television rarely allows the film-maker to work on the same film for a long period of time.

Perhaps direct cinema, in the sense in which Pennebaker and Perrault understand it – to mention only two extreme, exemplary cases – lies somewhere between cinema and television. Unfortunately it is certain that, unless an intelligent effort is made to reach a wider audience, this kind of cinema is condemned to go round in circles.

Herein, however, are the seeds of a revolution in the cinema. Let us take a few concrete examples.

The Forerunners

At the beginning of my essay, *Une Esthétique du réel, le cinéma direct,* I explained why I rejected the term *cinéma-vérité*, then used in America and often in Europe as well, to describe what direct cinema was dealing with.

The term was first used in France in 1961 to describe Jean Rouch's film *Chronique d'un Été*. This was based on an original idea conceived by Rouch and his co-director, the sociologist Edgar Morin. The film has certainly dated, but rather less than might be expected. Régis Debray appeared in it, looking rather unsure of himself, and also Jacques Rivette who, at the time, had made only *Paris Nous Appartient*. Jean Rouch, guided by the prolific Morin, chose a varied group of boys and girls at the

34

key point at which the postwar period was ending and the events of May 1968 – the rising of students and workers – were being hatched. Morin failed to consider deeply what he had said in his essay *Le Cinéma et l'homme imaginaire,* and this made him insert a rather embarrassing interview with an Italian girl into the film; the other youngsters were not noticeably decisive, either – they were discontented fringe people.

This very personal and special film of Jean Rouch's made French audiences feel that *cinéma-vérité* meant something inquisitorial, a kind of dustbin cinema. There was no real action in *Chronique d'un Été,* but a curious interaction between Edgar Morin, who at the time was involved in some personal crisis, and the others connected with the film, so that everyone, starting with the scriptwriter and his fellow director, stripped off a little bit. Here, the word *cinéma-vérité* really meant something. Yet there was a danger that people might think, as Morin himself did, that it was giving us *film-vérité* – the truth itself. At best, you could say it was putting out feelers; rather devilishly Jean Rouch, its director, produced a very personal and surprising film, reflected through his characters.

In their advertisements for the film, and during interviews, Morin and its producer, Anatole Dauman, referred to the *cinéma-vérité* of Dziga Vertov, the Kino-Pravda (from the name of *Pravda*) of the twenties. But there is a pretty slender relationship between this Soviet director and his followers. Georges Sadoul, in a remarkable article in a special number of *Image et Son* entitled 'Cinéma de la réalité'[1] (April 1965), explained that 'to Vertov, the cinema meant the structuration, through the editing, both of elements haphazardly found ("stock shots"), and of elements that could impose an air of chance upon life itself, by using, as a necessary preliminary, not a scenario (a word banned by the Kinoks), but a plan for the film's direction'. We know that Dziga Vertov experimented with talking pictures in *Enthusiasm* (or *The Donbass Symphony,* 1930) and in *Three Songs of Lenin.*

Luda and Jean Schnitzer, in their short monograph on Vertov, quote an important and previously unpublished

[1] This particularly full number also contains an important piece by Pierre Perrault and long extracts from an article by Louis Marcorelles entitled 'Le Cinéma direct Nord-Américain'.

declaration which he made in answer to the well-known manifesto of Eisenstein, Pudovkin and Alexandrov against realistic sound, and in support of the counterpointing of sound and image. It merely confirms Vertov's position:

'The declarations about the necessity of not coordinating sound and vision, whether they refer to films with "noises" or whether they refer to talking films, are not worth a fig. We make no distinction between sound cinema and silent cinema, merely between two kinds of film: documentaries (with real conversations, real noises, etc.) and acted films (with artificial conversations and noises, specially prepared for the film). Neither coordination, nor the lack of it, between sight and sound are obligatory, either for documentaries or for acted films. Sound sequences are made on the same principles as silent sequences; they can coincide or not coincide according to your editing and interweave in various necessary combinations.'

This admirably clear statement should remove all misunderstandings. Vertov considered himself a documentary filmmaker, and he made documentaries which he regarded in an almost religious way, as all the great documentary-makers of the time – Flaherty, Ivens, Grierson – regarded them. As time goes by, Dziga Vertov's films often seem closer to great silent Soviet cinema as a whole than to the documentary tradition, strictly speaking. When he was filming reality, Vertov never held the camera in his hand; this was something he left to his brother, Mikhail Kaufman. He never filmed in a 'neutral' way, but always sought the greatest degree of expressiveness by choosing the right angle at which to film his raw material. Sometimes his stylisation was a result of the angle from which he took his shots, sometimes the result of the quality of what was filmed; and the whole was coordinated by montage that was as capitally important to Vertov as it was to Eisenstein. The sound was gathered, and strictly arranged, in the same way. What Vertov considered *cinéma-vérité*, now, after all these years, seems merely a revolutionary determination to bear witness to the revolution by manipulating the revolutionary cinema. The Soviet critic M. P. Abramov quotes another admirable text of Vertov's, which reveals a vision of the world that is rare today: 'The realm in which I work is the most unexplored in the cinema. My methods demand superhuman efforts of organisation, technique, way of life and so on. It is the most thankless way to work. Believe me, it is really hard: Yet I hope that one day I shall achieve the victory of realism over formalism and naturalism, and become a poet who can be understood not by a few people, but by millions.' (*Premier Plan,* No. 35.)

The pre-eminence of realism over formalism and naturalism seems to be the one achievement gained from research into both 'direct cinema' and 'concrete cinema'.

Richard Leacock, D. A. Pennebaker and Albert Maysles carry on Vertov's work, not the letter of it, perhaps, but certainly its spirit; and to them the term *cinéma-vérité,* not translated into English, is both convenient and imaginative, and has none of the often unsatisfactory overtones it often has in France. It is the 'mirror' reflection of what Leacock is trying to do in relation to the established cinema, and of what Vertov sought in relation to it as well, that gives its whole meaning to the revolutionary direct cinema, which we hope to defend and illustrate. Vertov wanted truth, the whole truth, but not naturalism, and Leacock rejects the simulated realism of today's trendy directors. Besides, Vertov grew up and advanced in the days of the silent cinema, at a time when the present-day lightweight equipment was inconceivable. A change of quantity meant an abrupt change in quality.

Leacock, Perrault and others firmly refuse to be called documentary-makers, whereas Vertov, Flaherty, Ivens and Grierson were proud of the name; perhaps, today, it is no longer a term that seems alive and forceful. Thousands of bunglers have made the word come to mean a deadly, routine form of film-making, the kind an alienated consumer society might appear to deserve – the art of talking a great deal during a film, with a commentary imposed from outside, in order to say nothing and to show nothing.

Now, for images to speak through a tacked-on commentary is not enough. The film must speak for itself; but not like theatre, nor like literature.

The Revolution That Never Was[1]

Historically, Italian neo-realism in 1944–45, British 'free cinema' in 1956–59, and the French New Wave in 1958–59, show the first efforts that were made to create a cinema that was not costly, that came closer to reality, and that was free from slavery to technique. But, quite apart from their similarities or their differences, these three examples of a new kind of cinema all went ahead in a fairly consistent way – stylistically speaking – and started, either consciously or unconsciously, from quite definite premises which were quickly adopted by the more clear-sighted of those involved. Each movement (in the widest sense of the word) was quite clearly seeking to strip off the clichés and worn ideas, both in the cinema and in society. And the most significant films of the period bear on them, like a watermark, something that foreshadows the direct cinema of the sixties.

In Italy, fascism fell, and with it the well-oiled machine of the official cinema. After years of dictatorship there was a need to look straight at what was arising out of the ruins and wretchedness, and a few imaginative directors decided to comment on what was happening through a cinema that, willy-nilly, had to use whatever came to hand. They avoided stars and well-known faces; instead, they went out into the street and mixed with ordinary people. Above all, they were free of the heavy recording equipment of the studios, and this meant the first step towards freedom from the tyranny of 'tailored' film-making – that is, of directing in a closed, soundproof studio with marks on the floor to stop the actors taking a single unpremeditated step.

When, immediately after the war, Rossellini made *Rome, Open City* (1945) and *Paisà* (1946), the cinema began to look like one of Stendhal's notebooks. Unlike the synthetic films of Hollywood, Rossellini's films never tried to make people participate physically in what was happening; there was no dramatisation, no suspense in them. He made films where the action was actually taking place, using the people really

[1] See the essay already quoted, *Une Esthétique du réel, le cinéma direct.*

38

involved in this action or else actors who were not yet professionally smooth and so could identify themselves with ordinary people. He tried to show the small, grey, insignificant facts on the fringes of a great moment in history.

Vittorio De Sica, and Cesare Zavattini who wrote his scripts, took the film right in among the people. *Sciuscià* showed the abandoned children of Italy in 1946, tenderly and perhaps a little paternalistically. In *Bicycle Thieves*, a child again played an important part; but the character in the main role was played by a real worker. Although it is built up more dramatically, the action here is equally 'uncinematic'; De Sica, like Rossellini, tried to show the greyness of everyday life.

Out of necessity, film-makers went out into the street with lighter cameras but they lacked adequate sound recording equipment. Indeed, they made films without really bothering about the sound, which was dubbed in later by voices which were not, as a rule, those of the actors seen on the screen. Street sounds, all the environmental noises, could be added later as well; those were either pre-recorded sounds or else sounds taken down at the time. A major step had been taken by breaking with convention and filming outside the studio. But as far as sound was concerned, convention still ruled. The words used might be different from those of Hollywood or of fascist times; expressions, criticisms and profanities once forbidden in the name of respectability were heard. But the film-makers wanted their sound to be understandable, and so even non-professionals were dubbed and given more educated voices. At a later stage of neo-realism, Renato Castellani tried to keep the spontaneity of his original voices in *Two Pennyworth of Hope*. This was made in 1952 and was really the swansong of a period. But the dubbing was appalling: highly voluble people kept opening and shutting their mouths, equally excitable speech was heard, but any relationship between the movement of the lips and the words spoken was quite accidental. 'The dubbing', Richard Leacock, who admired the film a great deal remarked some time afterwards, 'was quite unlike the total spontaneity of the actors. The techniques used in the Italian style of direction', he said, 'meant that people could make films anywhere they pleased, without the slavery of heavy sound recording cameras and without being disturbed by unwanted

39

noises . . . But it was a spontaneity created by the skilful use of what I can only call an appalling technique.'

It was Luchino Visconti who first tried to listen to ordinary people and to make them speak out in their own surroundings and atmosphere. This was in *La Terra Trema* in 1948 and it was really revolutionary, despite the fact that it was a limited effort, marred by its uneasy attempts to symbolise the whole world's poverty in an excess of plastic delicacy. Visconti allowed his fishermen from Catania to express themselves in their own voices and their own dialect, and was accused of 'old-fashioned romanticism'[1] and 'retrograde language', since the script was inspired by Verga's *I Malavoglia*, which was written in educated Italian and not in dialect, seeing that he was a modern writer and free from rationalistic prejudices. The Italian critic Guiseppe Ferrara blamed what he called the 'reactionary purism' of left-wing circles that ought to have applauded what Visconti had done. 'Visconti's determination to keep pure the mother-tongue of the inhabitants of Aci-Trezza goes much further than any literary enthusiasm. It is first of all a kind of revenge against the reactionary purism that hates a cinema filled with dialect expressions, and it is therefore a victory for the language of humble people, of those who are never listened to, and in the end will express themselves without censorship and without false translations.' Today, *La Terra Trema* has dated because of its ideas of a systematic social hierarchy; but it is still important for its time because of this demand for direct sound, even though the clumsy 35 mm cameras made any freedom of movement impossible – as with Robert Flaherty's *Louisiana Story* made at about the same time. Visconti said at the time: 'I always film using direct sound. De Sica dubs his actors. But that's the end of everything, the whole meaning is lost.'

Ten years were to pass before Gian-Vittorio Baldi, in *La Casa delle Vedove* (The House of Widows), took over where Visconti had left off, and let old women talk quite freely, enhanced by very sophisticated colour but with a strict dramatic composition of its own. There the film returned to the classical cinema, but with a pinch of something else. It was in a short

---

[1] See Guiseppe Ferrara, *Luchino Visconti*, Editions Seghers.

film on an ethnographic subject, Gian-Franco Mingozzi's *La Tarenta*, in 1962, that direct sound was used in its most directly utilitarian sense. In his first full-length fiction film, *Trio* (1967), Mingozzi dealt with the life of three uncertain youngsters, two girls and a boy, who partly played themselves and were filmed 'directly'. The film, in 16 mm and with synchronised sound, was revolutionary for Italy, and gave a kind of dream-like life to a number of activities involving young people in Rome, such as a song festival or a large pacifist meeting at which the crowd broke into 'We shall overcome'. This film's lack of success sent Mingozzi back to good old traditional Italian dubbing. In 1967 Bernardo Bertolucci, with Baldi and a number of other young film-makers, declared war on the plague of dubbing and published a resounding manifesto on the subject.

This is a long way from countries like France and the United States, where films are always made with synchronised sound, even though it may be only a limited synchronisation, usually done entirely in the studio. It is a pity that Cesare Zavattini never faced up to the problem, for he was the theorist of neo-realism and became the fierce defender, at least before neo-realism died, of a cinema that came as close as possible to the reality of things. He had started as a writer and saw words as dead letters imprisoned in a book or a film script to be 'illustrated' by the cinema. I have hinted already at Vittorio de Sica's serious theoretical limitation: his natural bent towards the picturesque, the sentimental, the pretty. Rossellini, his extreme opposite, was often carried away by misty visions, so that his reality became more and more abstract and metaphysical; he brought shadowy outlines onto the screen, symbols of goodness and beauty. Had the rot already set in in his early films, in which dubbing was a necessity? However that may be, the circumstances around him later on did not help him to discover 'how things really are' as Bertolt Brecht expected the artist to do.

In 1945 Britain had the advantage over Italy of a long-established documentary tradition, and since 1939, of having made films that, although they might be rather static, kept well within this tradition, whether they were factual or fictional. Lindsay Anderson and Karel Reisz, who were to found 'free cinema', when they came to make film naturally took the only way open

41

to them – namely, documentary; and they did this both because they believed in it and because they wanted passionately to break into an industry that was closed to all newcomers. They used the documentary as a weapon against attitudes of Victorian puritanism still reigning in the early fifties, and speech played its part in this, with ordinary people being allowed to express themselves in their everyday language for the first time. Lindsay Anderson disliked naturalism, and in *Every Day Except Christmas* (1957), made in an extremely whimsical way for lack of light-weight sound-proof cameras, he flirted with synchronisation. The voices of porters and stallholders at Covent Garden could be heard, sometimes using crude words like 'bloody', which until then had been banned from the polite British screens; when the film was first shown commercially at the old Empire cinema in Leicester Square the audience gasped to hear people speaking naturally for the first time. Anderson could 'add' sounds and couple elements that were quite unlike one another; in fact he relied on language, on the psycho-social impact of familiar words. In 1953, with Guy Brenton, indoors and using direct sound he made *Thursday's Children*, a film about young deaf mutes at the Margate Institute. The spirit and style of this short film made it a remarkable example of direct cinema, although it achieved further emphasis through some pretty high-powered cutting. The subject certainly lent itself to such treatment, because the visual (movements of small children) dominated and the sound had a strong impact (stammered words when there were words at all). It did not make the audience break through the loneliness of these children, cut off from the world as they were, but it did give for a few minutes this feeling with unusual intensity.

Karel Reisz, the other pillar of free cinema, was equally conscious of the presence of sound. *We Are the Lambeth Boys* (1958) was the first film really conceived as 'living' cinema, the synchronised camera being present with a group of members of a youth club in a working-class district of London. Reisz, who wrote an important work called *The Technique of Film Editing*, achieved a good balance between discussions, dances, and external scenes, alternating serious, lively discussions in the club under the chairmanship of a leader with periods of work or

42

study. Reisz made his film in the old tradition, the story is 'set' in a particular place chosen for its special significance, for the meaning and emotion it arouses in the audience; it gives a rather grey and dull idea of the youngsters' lives yet is exciting for the images of them that appear in it.

Free cinema was officially born in 1956, within a programme of short and medium length films made by Anderson, Reisz and Tony Richardson. Today they are making fiction films. Free cinema belonged to a particular period of English history and became part of the general evolution of English culture which was equally apparent in the theatre and in the novel. There was a general effort to give the ordinary man a hearing: until then he had appeared on the stage or the screen only as a caricature. This complex, varied movement was embodied in the plays of Arnold Wesker, the early John Osborne, and Shelagh Delaney, as well as in the best films of the free cinema directors. In his famous novel *Saturday Night and Sunday Morning*, Alan Sillitoe created the character of a scoffing, vengeful young workman, Arthur Seaton, whose frank talk gave its special character to Karel Reisz's first full-length fiction film. Albert Finney, a north-country actor, immediately made his mark in it and for the first time in the British cinema the language and accent of the ordinary people of Nottingham was heard on the screen.

Since 1956 another revolution which is just as significant has taken place in Britain. A new generation of actors appeared in films and plays by these directors and playwrights, notably Albert Finney and Tom Courtenay, who no longer had to give up their original accents as actors in the past had done. In *This Sporting Life*, his first full-length fiction film made in 1963, Lindsay Anderson showed a way of life that was like that of *Saturday Night and Sunday Morning*, but in quite another tone – one that was non-realistic, indeed epic. His hero was a modern working-class man, whom Anderson, through an extremely subjective vision, exalted in his struggle to overcome established values. Once they came to make fiction films, Reisz and Anderson seemed to forget their earlier documentaries. But is this really true? Their documentaries came out of a particular moment in history, as a reaction against the conformity of the British cinema at the time, but they did not really break through into any kind of revelation, did not actually question the nature of reality. They merely scratched the surface of Victorian puritanism at the appropriate moment; their use of direct cinema was just an accident, it was not, in their case, a tool deliberately used to scrape off all the varnish of social convention.

Indeed, Lindsay Anderson actually declared that the films he made were in the classical tradition:

'I don't think that *real* sounds, and *real* dialogue are always as revealing or as interesting as *chosen* sounds . . . Looking back to *Every Day Except Christmas*, I don't think that a freer use of synchronised sound would have strengthened the film. In fact, it's that much more poetic because the sound isn't literal. When the boys are sitting in the café at night, chatting away, it's far more important to watch their faces than to listen to what they're saying; and the montage of sound effects and voices that accompany and rhythmically complete the montage of the voices selling in the market is more important to me than a sound-track linked to physical movements and lip movements could ever be.'

It would be hard to say more frankly that the cinema is essentially an art of photographic contemplation, reinforced by a few sound effects.

When it began, the French 'New Wave', personified by Claude Chabrol, François Truffaut and Jean-Luc Godard, in its efforts to free itself from the crushingly restrictive attitudes of the official industry, seemed to be moving towards the ideas of direct cinema. In order to film more freshly, these directors went out of the studio into the street or climbed about in real houses. Claude Chabrol did this in his first full-length film *Le Beau Serge,* which was filmed on location in the village he had adopted, with synchronised sound to cut down laboratory and synchronisation costs. Chabrol's is a heartfelt film, in which he kept to small revealing touches of provincial life, well observed, but picturesque. He began with a preconceived idea and refused to allow reality to speak for itself. After this he made films that became progressively more stylised, the actors playing in an exaggerated way that suited his particular tone. Even in his sketch *La Muette*, which was part of the collective

44

film *Paris vu par*, made in 16 mm with synchronised sound in 1966, he saw everything as outsize; direct cinema meant nothing to him.

Only François Truffaut in his first full-length film *Les Quatre Cents Coups* tried to make a really original film starting from the ideas of direct cinema. In the scene in which the young delinquent is interviewed at the reform school the camera concentrated on the face of Jean-Pierre Léaud who, at fourteen, was playing the leading part. Léaud was told to answer the psychologist's questions off the cuff. These questions were asked very quickly, and the boy replied at once, with very simple psychological reactions. Fast cutting accentuated the breathless atmosphere of the scene. Ten years later Truffaut used this young actor again and made him play the same character, Antoine Doinel, at the end of his military service, allowing Jean-Pierre Léaud great freedom to fill out the character and enrich the dialogue as far as the method, with synchronised sound, would allow it. *Baisers Volés* is a charming film, which, although modest and well observed, sticks closely to its fictional origins and never becomes more than entertaining. In it, direct cinema is used to come close to things, but not to reveal them.

From the time he made his short film *Charlotte et Son Jules* in 1958 with an actor who was then unknown, Jean-Paul Belmondo, Jean-Luc Godard has shown that he is much concerned with the text, the writing of the screenplay, and with various matters that suggested synchronous film-making. Of necessity he had to dub Belmondo, who was absent, and, through his own speech, showed a special care for cadence, rhythm, intonation and effect – all qualities quite contrary to realism. In *A Bout de Souffle*, his first full-length film, he used Belmondo once again, and insisted on non-realism, on psychological non-synchronisation, quite apart from the temporary non-synchronisation of the film-making method itself. Godard tried, more aggressively and more systematically than Lindsay Anderson, to stir things up as much as possible. In his third full-length film, *Une Femme est une Femme*, filmed with synchronised sound, he played about with the tone of voices, making a newsvendor sing, and modulating the exotic voice of his main actress, Anna Karina. We shall return again to this

45

provocative use of sound by French film-makers, which both limits their use of direct cinema and gives it its special originality.

As far as the French 'New Wave' was concerned, direct cinema was at first much more a matter of opportunism than of profound conviction. Their preoccupation with story-telling and performance, in the Balzac-like sense of the terms, meant that Truffaut and Chabrol had too rigid a framework to allow them to set aside the rules of the classical cinema. Like the Italians of the defunct neo-realism, the French 'New Wave' directors did not venture too far from the paths that led to the well-tried Hollywood models. This does not apply to Godard, who went his own way, and whose work shows certain similarities with that of Jean Rouch.

Richard Leacock

During the four years in which he collaborated with Robert Drew, the one-time journalist and producer, Richard Leacock – film enthusiast and cameraman – made about thirty films. Drew had been a reporter at *Life* Magazine. Leacock had photographed Robert Flaherty's *Louisiana story* in 1948 in a very classical style and Flaherty, his mentor, had urged him to go into film-making himself. Two million dollars, a more or less limitless sum, if Leacock is correct, was invested in the new enterprise by Time Inc. – the firm that publishes *Time* and *Life* – in the hope, according to Robert Drew, of 'creating a new form of film journalism'.

Between 1959 and 1963 anyone interested in direct cinema, from Chris Marker to young Americans seeking an adventurous form of film-making, visited the offices and cutting room of Drew Associates, then on 43rd Street, New York. Like an exterminating angel Richard Leacock buried all the old cinema in favour of a new 'spontaneous' cinema taken directly from reality. In a partly unpublished interview, extracts from which were published in London in the television magazine *Contrast* in the winter of 1964, he declared:

'I have become in a sense alarmed that with the development of cinema and television, we are all of us surrounded by images of things we don't know directly. What I mean is

46

this: I have for instance a great conviction within me that I know what happens in a law court. Now when I think about it, I've never in my life been in a law court: so I can't possibly know what happens in a law court. I've seen innumerable films and television shows which were very probably made by people who've never been in a law court either. And there are countless examples of this kind of thing. For instance, I was in Germany when Hitler came to power; and I know that what actually happened in no way resembled what I've seen in movies. I was in America when Pearl Harbor was invaded and I've seen subsequent films of this event, and they bear absolutely no resemblance to what I noticed. So that more and more we're building up an image of our society that is a fiction.'

Leacock went on to define very clearly what can be called his aesthetic code:

'Now in film-making, I have come from a tradition of controlled films (even though I worked a lot in documentary). Controlled films in the sense that we were recreating what a director thought the situation should be. I found more and more that I got bored with these recreations. Even if they were surprising, they were the product of somebody's imagination. They had nothing to do with what really happened. More and more as I made films of situations that were out of control, I found things that I thought extraordinarily interesting. Not because they were clever, or chic or anything, but because they were true. They presented you with data to try to figure out what the hell was really going on. What I think we're basically involved in doing is coming back to look at what's going on.

'Historically this is odd. When motion pictures were first invented, any smart person looking at them for the first time said: "Ah! Now we can capture life the way it really is" – Tolstoy for instance in 1907 said: "Now we can capture Russian life as it really is. We have no need any more to invent stories." The point was that in fact they couldn't; because the only way you can deal with human beings is to record the way they communicate, that is, talking; and the

47

other thing was that the equipment was so clumsy that the things all became a dreadful joke. Imagine moving in on a petrified housewife with cameras, lights, a crew and recording apparatus; tell her how to stand, how to speak, how to smile, how to relax and so on; and then ask her to be natural! What they really needed for that sort of film was competent actors! And so documentary, to my mind, had ceased to exist.

'Nothing could be done until the invention of the transistor, when sound and synchronising equipment became really portable. In 1960 we were able to make a camera which was silent, totally portable, and with sound that was separate and equally portable.'

Two films showed the originality of the methods pioneered by Richard Leacock – *Yanqui No!* and above all *Primary*. Both were made in collaboration with D. A. Pennebaker and Albert Maysles. *Yanqui No!* allowed people to hear Fidel Castro for the first time, soon after the Cuban revolution, speaking out of doors to an enthusiastic crowd, with the right sound reproduced, and to discover the poverty of yet another Latin-American country. No tendentious, propagandist commentary confused the presentation of the facts. Words, caught alive and on the spot, took on a special weight. Leacock and those who worked with him in a way showed up the nonsense Mikhail Romm was later to commit in 1965, in a film called *Ordinary Fascism*, which we shall return to; in this, Romm arbitrarily cut out the sound during Hitler's public speeches, filmed at the time, and thus left only his gestures which, not surprisingly, seemed grotesque. In this way he ignored what it must be admitted was Hitler's fascination over the German people, the verbal terror in which he held them. Leacock, on the other hand, plunged his audience straight into the Cuban crowd and, by using sound and words which were inseparable from the images, forced the audience to take part in what was happening. Leacock's images differ, for instance, from the Nazi classic, *Triumph des Willens* by Leni Reifenstahl, not just because the content of this film is radically opposed to that of the original German one, but because Leacock's style is so very different; it shows things familiarly, does not prettify things, the camera enters everyday life and removes the myths from it or, if it does

48

Richard Leacock's *Primary*, made in collaboration with
D. A. Pennebaker and Albert Maysles

D

show a myth, it extracts all it can from it and leaves the audience to draw its own conclusions.

This outlook of Leacock's appeared even more clearly in *Primary*, a film about the American primary elections of 1960 which led to the nomination of John F. Kennedy as the Democratic party candidate in the November elections, at the expense of future vice-president Hubert Humphrey. Leacock enjoys remembering what happened: for the first time in history a candidate went modestly looking for votes *in the street*, and shook hands with people passing on his own initiative. One scene deserves to become a classic because it illustrates the 'performance technique' side of things that immediately strikes the audience: it is the scene in which Kennedy and his wife Jacqueline go to a meeting of American Poles. The camera, held at arm's length by Albert Maysles, follows Kennedy pushing through the crowd to a small door at the end of the room which he must go through to get on to the platform. The words of the crowd are confused and seem addressed to the camera, which struggles physically to get to the platform, like Kennedy himself. A little later we watch the small movements of members of the Kennedy clan on the stage.

Today, television has plenty of facilities for this kind of reporting, and the technique used may seem quite ordinary. But then, although once the camera would show twisting hands, Leacock was not content to isolate a single detail arbitrarily, and later select it for special treatment at the cutting stage; on the contrary, he caught, *while it was happening*, the small revealing point, the sentence or part of a sentence that might throw light on a situation or a character, *the visual detail that cannot be treated separately from the sound that accompanies it.* This technique had never been used so rigorously before and it forces us to look at the cinema in an entirely new way, to redefine it in the way that Leacock, at his best, conceived it.

Several films illustrated this heroic period in which a new dimension in the cinema was discovered. The most remarkable is probably still *The Chair*, made in 1962. In the always revealing parts made by Leacock, in which we are taken to the very heart of a situation or a state of mind, particularly memorable are several moments during the trial of a black man condemned to the electric chair, when we see the reactions of his mother or
50

of this or that official; but, even more, the explosive joy of the defence lawyer, Louis Nizer, when he hears in his office that his client's sentence has been commuted, and the reaction of the condemned man himself to this same news, a little later. Occasionally, however, the cutting, which is rather too well aware of the effect it is seeking to make, spoils these pathetic scenes, with their sense of the arbitrariness of human justice.

Leacock stresses the didactic value of his films in the strong, almost Brechtian sense of the word. In the interview from which we quoted earlier he says:

'Surely you don't want a single reaction of an audience. I go back to education. I did a film on crystals once (I used to be a physicist, and I love physics; it is as exciting as any form of theatre); and one of the most important shots (to me) I've ever made was made through a microscope. It was a shot of a crystal, a very beautiful crystal. We melted down this crystal under a microscope until it was just a little wiggly crescent moon, a single blob of nothing, no definable shape. And then we allowed it to grow under the microscope, not heating it any more. It grew very, very fast on the inside and very slowly on the outside, until it became sort of round, and then it became square; and suddenly it went click, click, click, click; and four absolutely perfectly straight sides moved outwards. And you can show that shot to people . . . I showed it to an old man in a lab – an old man who inspects film for scratches, who looks at miles of film – and when he saw this he gasped; he said, "My God, what happened?" If you can do this in education . . . where, in a class of a hundred children, perhaps three of those children will go to a library and try and find out then you've had a profound effect on those three. You're never going to have a film where you get a hundred children going to the library to find out what's happened.'

This wish to respect reality in an integral way, and at the same time to make the audience think, lies at the heart of Leacock's method, which is ambitious enough to be compared with Bertolt Brecht's methods in the theatre, and his idea of the

51

'epic'. Later we shall study the respective influence of these two men on the actor, either professional or non-professional, and the way in which the audience sees his performance. In both cases it is a matter of looking critically at reality, but in an aesthetic, not a literal or a naturalistic way. Brecht, limited by the four walls of the stage even when they opened on to broad horizons, tried to make the flow of events understandable – a flow he put across with a number of techniques: narrative, décor, and scenic effects. The audience always bears in mind the fact that it is in the theatre, that what it sees is stylised, that what it sees is not real life but its reflection through the theatre, and so that it must never let itself identify with what it is seeing and hearing. Its own emotions will reveal what Brecht liked to call 'the true state of things'.

In the theatre, even, indeed particularly, in Brecht's plays, (that is, in the performances of the Berliner Ensemble, given during his lifetime and after his death), which are at the very boundary of our whole theatrical tradition, nothing is true at the start except the flesh-and-blood actors, and the wood and fabrics of the décor and the accessories. All one remembers about the décor is some quintessential point – a mark to show that things have become worn by time, some rich fabric to show a particular, precise social setting. The actors refuse to use effects and tricks and keep *composing*, in the strongest sense of the word, through their elocution, delivery, gestures, bearing and looks, seeking above all to fill each moment of their performance with a clear reference to the *real*. This reality, although it is a selected reality, chosen by Brecht according to his critical way of looking at things, does not appear at the start but is invariably seen at the end. In the cinema, and particularly in the films of Richard Leacock, reality is achieved from the start through realism, or rather through the naturalism of the synchronous image. The great mobility of the sometimes shaky camera adds to the intense feeling the spectator has of participating in, and so of identifying with, the people and the events described. Miles of film are shot 'live', and this raw material has to find a meaning when it is cut; but it must be cut in a way that does not alter the spirit of the direction.

Success should mean that the spectator is so provoked that he loses his self-confidence and, by an exactly opposite attitude,
52

arrives at the essential part of Brecht's message: that nothing must ever be considered as 'moving on its own'.

In 1963, Leacock parted from his first associate, Robert Drew, who had sometimes imposed his conception of a style of editing that was too much concerned with the immediate effect of the film and so, inevitably, produced simplification. Leacock formed his own production company with D. A. Pennebaker to continue his fundamental search for what was central, essential; seeking not so much for 'bloody' reality as for 'living' reality in the strongest sense of the word. He tried to discover just what lay behind the apparently united fabric of the familiar, everyday world, and in so doing, he hoped to go even further towards Brecht's attitude. From then onwards he had to work more economically, to 'cobble' a film together on twenty thousand rather than the hundred thousand dollars he had had in his Drew Associates days. This gave him the ideal working conditions, and the enormous problems they produced, which he had defined when he started working with direct cinema in 1959. They were two people – the cameraman and the girl who recorded the sound. Here he recalls how he made his first independent film:

'*Quint City, U.S.A.* was made entirely by myself, with one very small girl who has the advantage that I can always shoot over her. The two of us, in three weeks, shot the entire film, and we never asked anybody anything or to do anything. We were simply observers. You can't have a director with this kind of film. You even have to edit your film as the event is actually happening. You have to decide: it's this and this and this I want to look at; and not this and this and this. And you can't sit there wondering, what does the director want me to do. You have to make the decisions yourself; you can't alter anything afterwards; nothing can be reshot. You're doing an entirely different thing: you're a social observer. Your own ingenuity becomes less important than the fact of how interesting the subject is; and whether your own approach to it is interesting enough. You don't show the whole of a subject; you select; and your selection matters.

'And after you've shot it, the same things are true of the editing. You can't hand the stuff over to someone else to edit;

53

the idea is grotesque. Only you know what happened. Time and again I've seen material where the really important moment in a scene is a tiny, tiny fragment of the whole bulk of the footage. If you hand it over to an editor, he will be impressed by the bulk and miss this tiny fragment. You have to do it yourself. You see, this sort of film has really very little to do with classical motion-picture making.'

And before leaving the subject it may be useful to recall what Leacock told me immediately afterwards about 'classical' cinema, because it shows the complete break between cinema as it is conceived today and 'new cinema' in the full meaning of the term as Leacock would like to see it.

'The last classical picture I worked on was *Baby Doll*,[1] with Kazan. He's a marvellous director to work with – a challenging, interesting, fabulous guy – but basically you're an illuminating engineer. How do you want your bathroom lit? Do you want your hallways with moonlight, sunlight, fog, rain, snow? You can do six a day. You can get fascinated by putting little shadows here and there on the wall and having curtains move a little bit . . . To me, it's boring. I've seen a marvellous description in a book of how to light a death scene. It says that "The window should be slightly open and, as the loved one expires, there should be a gentle gust of wind, the curtain should move slightly." Most touching. It's a book called *Painting with Light* which also tells you when shooting westerns to use real Indians if possible; but if Indians are not available, use Hungarians . . .'

Leacock may have risked exaggerating a little when he gave his views on the traditional cinema, but he described very clearly a general system in which everything is based on lack of authenticity. If only the profiles of performers are used, then a Hungarian is as good as an Indian. Laszlo Szabo, for instance,

[1] Richard Leacock helped Kazan, anonymously, to re-shoot two or three parts of the film since Boris Kaufman, the cameraman, was no longer available.

played an Arab in some of Godard's films (*Le Petit Soldat* and *Weekend*); these Arabs were not seen in depth – how they spoke and breathed; all that was shown was certain mannerisms they were supposed to have, and a particular appearance. The fact that Laszlo Szabo is an infinitely more complex character than this schematic attitude suggests raises the whole problem of realism, of the film actor's physical presence. A more subtle and no less characteristic example is the performance by the American Burt Lancaster of the hero of Luchino Visconti's film *The Leopard*. In the original Italian version, dubbed, as always happens in Italy, a balance was achieved in the character through a wise difference between the physical presence of this well-known actor and the excellent way in which he was dubbed by a professional Italian actor. The result was a fine spectacle but, I must stress, only the *outline* of a Leopard, neither the actor, nor the character he was playing, being present in any kind of depth.

Indeed, if you take it as far as it will go, further even than Leacock's own ideas, direct cinema involves questioning the whole technique of the actor's performance; first of all, what he is at the start, his affinity with the character he is playing, what he may become, and by what method he will come to evolve in that particular way. At this point something that Leacock said seems crucially important; he is talking about communication with the person or persons who are to be filmed, and what he says applies equally well to the dramatic cinema as it does to filmed interviews, at times the most banal kind of cinema there is and the standby of so many 'direct' programmes on television.

'I want to discover something about people. When you interview someone they always tell you what they want you to know about them. This may be interesting, and is what some people actually want to record. What I want to see is what happens when they are not doing this. Now this is very difficult. I know a wonderful, hilarious woman in Aberdeen, South Dakota.[1] A wonderful nun who runs the house of a

---

[1] This was the small town used in *Quint City, U.S.A.*, which we shall deal with in detail later.

lawyer. She's tough, witty, a marvellous character. But the moment you turn on a camera, she becomes the public's view of a nun, saintly, sweet, no bite to her tongue. Turn on the camera and she changes. My problem with her would be to hang around long enough – two, three, maybe four days – until you fade away, and she is faced with a situation which shows her as she really is. You could interview her for weeks and weeks and weeks and she'd remain the saintly image of a nun.

'There are certain very obvious people in our society of course who act roles. A judge, for instance. At home he's just a mortal, with all the difficulties and aches and pains and bills to be paid of any other mortal. But somewhere, between leaving home and walking into court in his robes, he changes and becomes a totally different person. It's a real change. He's not faking. He really becomes a different person. A great conductor in America used to say this: somewhere between leaving his home and arriving at Symphony Hall, Kussevitsky had to become Eroica. If they were to perform Eroica, no matter how sick he was, how depressed, when he walked on to that platform, he had to *be* Eroica. By the tiniest gestures he had to convey that. Now this is true also of average people. Some average people have very large responsibilities, you know. Very few people can imagine what it feels like to drive an express train. There are all sorts of jobs.'

Two fundamental criticisms of Leacock's films have been made, and the two really come to the same thing, because they are both to do with the quality of what is received through the 'living camera' (as Drew and Leacock at first called their work). First of all, the director tries not to interfere with the subject or subjects he is filming. He tries to be a perfectly objective 'social observer' who has managed to be so completely accepted by his surroundings and by the people in them that he is really quite unnoticed. Is this possible? It leads to the second criticism: the very fact that a man is filming reality means that he is altering the contents of reality, choosing parts of that reality which automatically express a very particular position and point of view. Godard criticised Leacock in this way in the text we quoted earlier. Leacock replies to the first criticism:[1]

'One of my suspicions is that without thinking we have been copying the pretensions and the rules of dramatic film. We have been assuming, for instance, that we are not really there. We have been making these assumptions because we have not really thought through what should be our relationship to what's happening. We have to do some experimenting. We don't really know.

'Pennebaker and I were out in a snowstorm. We were making a tyre commercial for television because we needed some money. And some very interesting situations took place which were absolutely wild – and we were accidentally filming. You know, people got out of cars and related to the camera in a way that when we saw it on the screen, it wasn't any use to us, but it was electrifying. Everybody's thought of using the camera in the first person, but it's never really worked before because it's always been too much of a mechanical gadget. But here people actually were relating to the camera. There's one lovely scene where a lady gets out of a car in a howling snowstorm and offers it a cookie. And the camera accepts . . . What we were doing that day was social observations; then you explore these kinds of techniques according to a gradation that goes from pure social observation right back to true dramatic cinema.'

Leacock refutes Godard's point that the facts themselves are deceptive quite without meaning to be so,[2] in a way that clearly reveals his fundamental scientific obsession; this, once again, goes back to Brecht's effort to create the 'art of the scientific century' in the theatre. I quote:

'This is the argument that is constantly brought up by people who have read too little philosophy . . . people who are very

[1] *L'Esthétique du direct,* p. 33. This alludes to the 'dramatised' films, made when he was working with Drew, such as *The Chair.*
[2] After saying this, Godard directed in the streets of New York, in November 1968, with D. A. Pennebaker at the camera.

naïve and have no knowledge of scientific techniques and the philosophy of modern science and get very excited by the fact that when you introduce a camera into a situation you change it. Now this is a very old problem, and at this point not a very interesting one, to anyone at least who is at all interested in the philosophy of science. A physicist, when he examines something – a crystal, say, in which you want to measure the electrical potential between one point and another. You apply a volt meter. The moment you apply that volt meter, you change the circuitry of that crystal. Every scientist knows this. Knowing this, you make a volt meter which changes it as little as possible . . .

'Now, if there are a thousand people in a room and a newspaper reporter enters that room he changes the situation very little. If there's just one person in a room and a newspaper man enters that room he changes the situation much more. You are aware of this. The same is true of the camera. Of course it changes the situation. The question is how much does it change it. You have to be aware of this, you have to sense it.'

The duality that can be found in Leacock's thought between the search for an almost objective rendering of the event, and the chances of interpretation offered by both direction and cutting, is not as contradictory as it may seem if it is analysed in the light of two films he made, with a girl helper who did the cutting, after 1963 when he broke with Drew Associates and formed his own company, Leacock-Pennebaker: *Quint City, U.S.A.* (1964) and *Igor Stravinsky, a Portrait* (1966). *Quint City, U.S.A.*, which is also known as *Happy Mother's Day*, satirically shows the birth of quins in a modest farming family in a small Middle West town – Aberdeen, South Dakota. Aberdeen becomes the centre of the world, or at least of the United States; presents and advertising offers pour in without affecting the solidly sensible couple at all. Leacock played on the contrast between the crazy goings-on around her and the olympian calm of Ma Fisher and, though he appeared to be perfectly objective, he had no difficulty in showing the absurdity of this contradictory advertising farce in American society – the kind of thing that Elia Kazan tried to show in his famous *A*

Face in the Crowd (scriptwriter: Budd Schulberg). The camera is a microscope, yet a microscope that must be carried, twenty pounds of it, at arm's length. It pokes its way into the action, into the intimate details of families like the Fishers (the child crooning over five new-born kittens; the trip around the farmyard in the old car, or into confrontations with society – the shopping trip to buy clothes; Mrs Fisher on the stage of honour in the little town, watching, pop-eyed, a parade in her honour). A young woman who has made a number of direct cinema films, Patricia Jaffe, says in an excellent article[1] on the cutting of this type of film: 'When you have marvellous direction (like Leacock's in this film) you can show the film almost as it came out of the camera . . . It has the quality and rhythm of a ballet and whole sequences can be left as they are.' *Quint City, U.S.A.* shows the furthest point to which Leacock took his technique and is a real exercise of style because, without using contortions of the camera, special effects, rare angles or cutting tricks, the material speaks for itself and reveals an amazing human comedy that tells us more about America than dozens of other films. It is up to the spectator to make up his own mind.

Leacock's next film was just the opposite of this. *Igor Stravinsky, a Portrait*, cut by Leacock from the material of the programmes filmed by him but made in collaboration with the musicologist Rolf Lieberman for the *Norddeutsch Rundfunk* of Hamburg, refused to be at all dramatic, even when the situation would quite naturally allow it to be, as it did in the case of *Quint City, U.S.A.* The shots taken by Leacock, with a young assistant, Sarah Hudson, who recorded the sound and took part in the cutting, show Stravinsky at work and with other people, talking constantly about his art and about music. The camera takes us around Beverly Hills, Hamburg and London, shows him meeting Pierre Boulez, Nicholas Nabokov, Christopher Isherwood and, in particular, George Balanchine accompanied by the young star of the New York City Ballet, Susan Farrell. Instead of being plain reporting, to use the rather contemptuous term people apply to nearly all direct cinema (often described

'Editing *cinéma vérité*', *Film Comment*, New York, Summer 1965. '*Cinéma vérité*' is used here to mean 'direct cinema'.

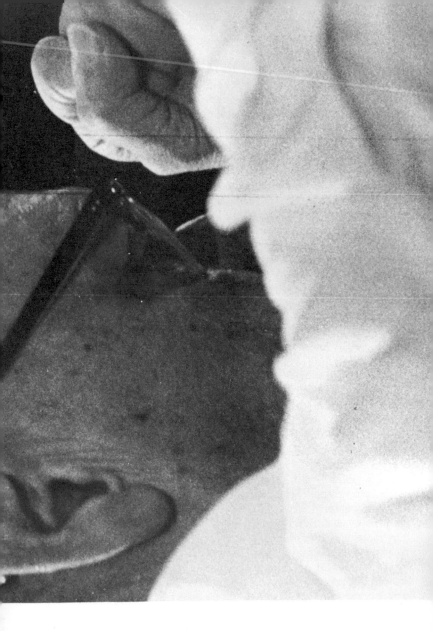

Richard Leacock's *Igor Stravinsky, a Portrait*

as 'unartistic' since it is aiming to be something else), *Igor Stravinsky, a Portrait* becomes, profoundly, radically and quintessentially, a work like that of Mallarmé, if I may dare to say so, a poetic reflection on art and on creation, and at the same time a film whose style most clearly reveals the character of Stravinsky.

Stravinsky lived only for his art, for art generally, and for the meaning of art. Leacock's camera had only one object, to catch this constant palpitating sense of artistic creation. The very opening, with Pierre Boulez scurrying around the composer, gives us an image of the novice, of someone trying to make an effect whereas Stravinsky shows absolute mastery. Stravinsky not only lived for art, but lived in art. In London he meets Balanchine accompanied by Susan Farrell. A discussion takes place, on the *Variations in Memory of Huxley* which, it seems to me, is gradually transformed into dancing steps by the fair, diaphanous dancer. Stravinsky remarks: 'Our feeling is more right than our calculations.' The steps are inscribed in space (fairly small, it seems), improvised, born from a single feeling, controlled by acquired discipline and the rhythm of the dance. In a corner of the image we see George Balanchine, deep in the admiration a connoisseur feels for his favourite pupil. For a moment it looks as if Degas has become animated; the whole genius of the cinema, and the sensitivity of a delicate artist making the most of this new medium still in infancy, have come together. A few seconds of eternity, like no others: an example of perfect cinema, image, sound and movement in absolute unity.

Stravinsky, citizen of the world, cosmopolitan artist: much of Leacock's film is a play on words and languages as a kind of profession of faith on the part of Stravinsky, who used them. In speaking, Stravinksy keeps passing from English to German and sometimes to French, occasionally adding a word or two in Russian: 'I am not so lucky as *böse*' (*böse* is German); 'I adore dissonance, consonance *ist viel schwerer*.' Thus he speaks a synthetic language borrowing from different countries, with an ill-defined, rather emphatic accent. Each word, whether English, French or German, is there for its rhythmical values, its tone, and its plastic values, and he does not worry about grammar. Only the Russian sounds authentic. The life of the

61

Jane Fonda in *Jane* by D. A. Pennebaker
Bob Dylan in *Don't Look Back* by D. A. Pennebaker

man who composed 'The Rite of Spring' could best be described by the title of Stanislavski's book – *My Life in Art*. The last sentence spoken in the film – its meaning, its colour, its emotive power – is a poem in itself and sums up the spirit of a film which is, I think, one of the finest and newest in the whole history of the cinema: 'I am waiting, all my life,' with a very diphthonged 'w' that is characteristic of Stravinsky's pronunciation. Anyone who has not seen *Igor Stravinsky, a Portrait*, who has not undergone this intense experience, cannot, I think, know what the words 'direct cinema', as I have tried to define them in this essay, really mean.

Richard Leacock's radical originality has left little room for analysis of his equally important colleague, D. A. Pennebaker, who made *Jane*, about Jane Fonda, *David*, about a young drug addict undergoing a cure at Synanon in California, and more recently *Don't Look Back* on Bob Dylan and *Monterey Pop* on the hippies' pop festival at Monterey. What Pennebaker seeks above all is rhythm and rhythmical relationships, and he pushes almost to absurd lengths Leacock's revolutionary discoveries. One must be entirely 'in', participate in depth. Albert Maysles, who began with Leacock and Pennebaker, today works only with his brother David who designs the films he photographs. Albert Maysles is a virtuoso who can do anything with a camera and is at his best in producing an atmosphere (Ringo's dance at the Peppermint Club in Times Square in *The Beatles in New York*, for instance, or the producer Joseph Levine visiting friends he had known as a poor boy in Boston, in *Showman*). Language becomes an exciting mixture of expressions, flung out spontaneously; and it confirms the fact that there has been a revolution in sound.

Salesman, in 1969, was the Maysles brothers' most ambitious film. This followed the day-to-day life of four Bible salesmen in New England and Florida. Albert Maysles and his brother once studied psychology and they quote with conviction this sentence of Francis Bacon, which Albert Maysles would happily make his *credo*: 'The contemplation of things as they are, without error or confusion, without substitution or imposture, is in itself a nobler thing than a whole harvest of invention.' Unlike Richard Leacock, Albert Maysles did not hesitate to venture forth on a full-length film describing lives that quite clearly had

63

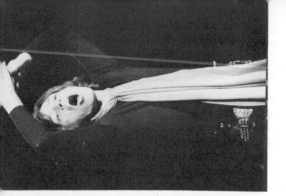

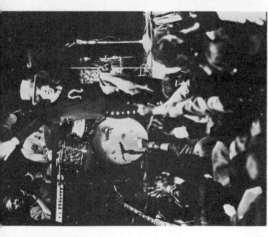

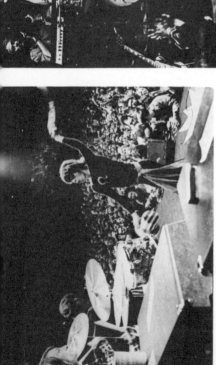

The Rolling Stones in *Gimme Shelter* by David and
Albert Maysles and Charlotte Zwerin

no story as such, and in a sense he produced the kind of testimony that Arthur Miller sought in his famous play, ideally accomplishing his purpose, as Miller himself was quite ready to admit. David Maysles who, with Charlotte Zwerin, was responsible for the cutting, emphasised a kind of fatality in the way the mechanics of social life crush defenceless people, and he showed the daily routine perfectly. A less literal presentation, and a clear awareness that reality is never innocent but belongs in a wider context, might have given this patient, loving film the critical dimension without which it remains merely a remarkable exercise in style.

This is the place to mention two very well-known outsiders: Shirley Clarke, who once worked with Leacock and persuaded a black transvestite to talk for two hours between four walls in *Portrait of Jason*; and Andy Warhol, who made *Chelsea Girls*, in which, on two more or less 'interlocked' screens, we are shown tableaux of the customs of the strange occupants of a famous hotel in New York. Here, direct cinema allows a kind of delayed reaction in time: it is not a revelation in the immediate present.

Pierre Perrault

Richard Leacock might be called *homo cinematographicus par excellence*, but Pierre Perrault, who came to the cinema from literature, through the tape-recorder and television, is his exact opposite. He brings to film-making a strictly critical eye that knows nothing of the established rules, and whereas Leacock makes the cinema burst out from within, from its most fundamental structures (the camera and sound recording, to start with), Perrault feels that these things can be taken for granted. He sees them merely as tools that will give a certain permanence to the extremely interesting work he has been carrying on for ten years in his own country – that is, the province of Quebec, studying its mainly French-speaking people and their paradoxical fate in an English-speaking Canada. Leacock brought the surgeon's knife to reality and sought to reveal man's innermost secrets in the passing moment, whereas Pierre Perrault, instead of writing novels or an epic poem, finds echoes of something greater in what appear to be the banal

E   65 reality of modest people's everyday lives: this greater quality being the growth of a sense of unity.

When he worked on his first full-length film, *Pour la Suite du Monde* (following a series of a dozen half-hour films entitled *Au Pays de Neufve France*, made by René Bonnière), Pierre Perrault shared the responsibility of direction with his cameraman, Michel Brault. Brault, who was familiar with the techniques of Leacock, Pennebaker and Maysles but also interested in the classical cinema, is ready to do anything anywhere, no matter what the style. For him, the subject orders the technique, not vice versa, as in Leacock's case. Direct cinema, as I have tried to show through considering Leacock, means more than a light camera and synchronised sound; it demands immediate participation in the event. The performance does not come only from the text, even though this may be constantly improvised: it comes from the very movement of the action itself, with a minimum of interference from the direction team. Ideally the director is his own cameraman, he shares the physical effort of seeking what is real, sticks to the movement of things and of people as it is actually taking place by physical contact, that is, the contact of the camera with reality, and of the director-sound-man with the camera. This is not the camera used as a mere gadget, the way Claude Lelouch uses it when he dances around his characters on the station platform at the end of *Un Homme et une Femme*, to express their joy at meeting again through this wild movement. Leacock definitely cuts out symbolism. Here the '*caméra-stylo*' which Alexandre Astruc spoke about, but which was then merely a publicity stunt to make people realise that films could be 'written' like novels, came into being, perhaps for the first time, although now it was not a matter of writing novels in the form of films but quite simply of making films. Not *as well as* novels, with the extra excitement of the classic 35 mm camera, but in *another way*: a new way of seeing, hearing, feeling, with a refinement of feeling that enriches all our perception, all our understanding of the world.

Pierre Perrault's break with the classical cinema, and with the whole tradition of direct cinema as it already existed in Canada – a tradition inspired by what was happening in New York at about the same time –·showed unusual boldness and originality from the outset. Direct cinema in Canada was at first the work of an English team in the National Film Board, the cradle of all Canadian film making. A label was attached to it: 'candid eye', which in itself covered everything that was done, because the accent was placed on the eye's candour, the implication being that it concentrated on some primal innocence unspoiled by intervention from outside. Although I have tried hard to find who first used this label I have not been able to do so; it may have been the team of Wolf Koenig-Roman Kroitor, or the Englishman Terence McCartney-Filgate.

In a special brochure of the Canadian *Cinémathèque*, published in 1967, Wolf Koenig says that the idea of the 'candid eye' comes from a British film made by Lindsay Anderson, the creator of 'free cinema'. This film, *Thursday's Children*, made a strong impression on Koenig and his friends in the English-speaking team, an impression even stronger than that made by Flaherty's old films or the English documentaries of the thirties. 'All these films,' he wrote, 'had the colour of reality, the colour we wished to give to what we were doing.' Just then television broke through the American market, and the National Film Board of Canada was told to provide the newly-formed television branch of Radio Canada with films. 'We thought this was the chance we had been waiting for: there was an audience, and there was a budget . . . This was what we meant to do: catch life as it was, without a script and without frills; take sound on the spot, without careful cutting; make films in a way that would create emotion, laughter or tears, and preferably both at once; show them on television to millions of people and change the world by making them see that life is true, fine and full of meaning.' In 1953, Wolf Koenig was given Henri Cartier-Bresson's book of photographs *Images à la sauvette*, the preface of which, he said, was to become the bible of the whole 'candid eye' team. I cannot quote the whole long passage which Koenig quoted in an article about the Canadian documentary, but will recall this important and contradictory sentence in the context of direct cinema: 'To me a photograph is a simultaneous discovery, in a fraction of a second, partly of the meaning of a fact, and partly of a rigorous arrangement of the forms, visually perceived, which express that fact.' The conclusion follows that: 'It is in living that we discover

67

ourselves, at the same time that we discover the world outside. It shapes us, but we cannot work on it in the same way. A balance must be established between these two worlds, the inner and the outer worlds that are really a single one, in a conscious dialogue with each other; and it is this world that we must communicate.'

In the first extract there is a contradiction in the extent to which the author believes that what is happening is caught 'alive' and at the same time 'composed'. What is possible in the field of photography with a very light camera and without the use of sound is not possible in direct cinema, of which the 'candid eye' is only a variant. As for the conclusion, it expresses a laudible but purely theoretical ambition, and nothing is said about the way it is to be realised. *Lonely Boy* (1963), a film about the pop-singer Paul Anka, shows the limitations of the vision of Koenig and Kroitor: even by small manipulations of the sound they quickly managed to emphasise the caricaturish element in their subject. In another of their films, another one on Igor Stravinsky of which I have only seen the French version, the insufficiency of the 'candid eye' is clearly revealed: it *is* merely 'candid', taking images and words quite at random. A photograph has to render an account to no one except itself. But moving photographs are quite different. The fact that they are linked to one another presupposes a moral standpoint, a moral relationship that has nothing to do with ordinary good-will. The material filmed must be seized and made to give up its essential being, its pith, its deepest meaning. *Lonely Boy* is about level with a good piece of magazine reporting, the kind of thing that turns up in *Life* or *Paris-Match*. The film on Stravinsky, which demands more ambitious treatment, shows only the triumph of the feeble, gossipy incident, and is all the more disappointing in comparison with the film made by Richard Leacock during the same period. Visibly, no communication is established between the film-makers and their subject.

What went wrong from the start was the fact that sound was thought unimportant. Sound, in the films of Koenig and Kroitor, completes the image; it does not form part of it as in Leacock's films and in those which Pierre Perrault made later with a completely different attitude and quite other

68

ambitions. It is worth going back once more to the interview with Richard Leacock which has already been quoted extensively:

'We have a great problem with the people we work with. There's a great emphasis on the camera, which in our situations does become a dominating thing. Now all the people who have worked with us tend to think of themselves in a derogatory sense when they are recording sound and keep thinking: "If only I was running the camera." Funnily enough this annoyed both Pennebaker and myself to such an extent that the last time we went out shooting we went out together and we alternated the whole time according to the situation we were in. We kept changing sides. We've never found anyone who really devotes himself to recording sound; but recording sound is just as interesting as shooting. You've got to raise your sights, and realise the incredible importance of getting the sound right. At the moment it's not a technical problem, it's a human problem. You have to think of sound and image as two cameras with two quite different problems.'

It is almost possible to speak of the 'dramatic art' of sound recording; the sound-man must know how to place himself, how to move in the particular situation and among those particular characters. Obviously Sarah Hudson, who was in charge of sound recording for *Igor Stravinsky, a Portrait* and later helped with the cutting, helped to give the film a quality, a warmth, an intensity, that Koenig and Kroitor's film on Stravinsky totally lacked. Two people managed to make a masterpiece, whereas in the Canadian film a dozen failed to do so.

Another member of the original 'candid eye' group is Terence McCartney-Filgate, an Englishman who is his own cameraman and sometimes his own sound recorder as well, and who deserves credit for having lent all his talent to the sound revolution. He made two films in 1958 and 1959, *Blood and Fire*, about the Salvation Army, and *Days before Christmas*, about the coming of Christmas in Montreal; Michel Brault and George Dufaux from the French team collaborated, and so did

69

Wolfe Koenig. 'It was Filgate,' Brault said, 'who urged me to hold the camera in my hand, and to give up the tripod.' The main scene in *Blood and Fire* takes us to a meeting of repentant sinners: we hear the confessions pouring out, the voices' intonation betraying the sinners' feelings. No one cares about the presence of the camera or the sound. In *Days before Christmas* Father Christmas talks to children in a big store and listens to their ingenuous confidences.

But it was only in *Back-breaking Leaf*, a little later, that Terence McCartney-Filgate freed himself from a still 'candid' idea of sound, as one spoke about the 'candid camera', and gave us a glimpse of its full aesthetic possibilities. In the publication of the Canadian *Cinémathèque*, Marcel Carrière who, for a long time, before he went on to direction, was head of sound in the National Film Board of Canada, and also worked with English teams (*Lonely Boy*) and French ones (*Pour la Suite du Monde*), explains the role of sound in direct cinema very clearly, although he uses a rather *simpliste* example. He takes the case of a lorry on the road: 'In *cinéma-vérité*,'[1] he says, 'all you hear is the engine: in post-synchronisation all you hear is the dialogue (the scene might just as well have taken place in a drawing room).' He might have added that in the classical cinema, whether the sound is synchronous or dubbed, the object is always to get sound that is filtered as much as possible, purified of all its surroundings, a sound in which only the dialogue (spoken, as a rule, by professional actors) dominates, and has a clarity that cuts out all the hesitations, uncertainties and doubts of real life. Acting is in a single register, and the technique officially caught in the cinema schools is a slave to this absurd demand. *Back-breaking Leaf* is about tobacco picking in Ontario, and in it McCartney-Filgate was responsible for the sound recording as well as the general direction, helped by the camera of Gilles Gascon. The treatment of the subject clearly suggests social criticism in its picture of the day-labourer selling his muscular strength to earn a living in the summer (a reminder of John Steinbeck's *The Grapes of Wrath*). In an entirely unliterary way, through language and sound in movement, we are shown the alienation involved in this work.

[1] Here, the term is used with its American meaning.

It is time to hire workers, the men turn up and a woman explains that they will have to do their best. Tobacco picking starts, the leaves rustle, they must be picked then tied together. Under a veranda a man is groaning, he has drunk water that has made him ill. In the morning the men set off through the mist of Norfolk County to the clop of horses' hooves. Then comes work in the rain, backs bent; and then the return along the slushy roads, the sound of footsteps in water. We *see* and *hear* these men's labour, as far as sound expressionism can take us. Possibly Filgate was trying to say too much, like his friends of the 'candid eye'; but this does not prove that the role of sound in the living cinema is any less important. Besides, he makes people speak to criticise society rather as 'free cinema' did, or rather he denounces society merely by the weight of meaning in their words, which the structuralists call its connotation.

At the time of *Days before Christmas* the French Canadians at the National Film Board in Canada began to make their own films; the first of these was *Les Raquetteurs* made by Michel Brault and Gilles Groulx in 1958. It was made in 35mm with synchronised sound, and with cruel irony it shows the odd behaviour of a dressed-up crowd taking part in a curious competition in Montreal. We laugh at these respectable middle-class people with their candid reactions (the 'candid eye' is very close), all muffled up in their warm winter clothes, and talking French in their own very special accent. This was the first time French Canadians had been shown directly on the screen. In 1961 Gilles Groulx made a film on his own, *Golden Gloves*, about a famous boxing competition. It was the chance to make Ronald Jones, a black boxer, well known. He had made his home, obscurely, in the poorest French district and spoke French at home and English in his boxing world; and he went through the series that led to the Golden Gloves contest which promised riches and success. Groulx was already showing a dual interest that was to make him, with Pierre Perrault, the most personal film-maker in Quebec: on the one hand he used direct sound knowledgeably, as in the opening of the film where we watch the boxer in training; on the other, he was commenting on a precise social situation – showing how a man here boxed in order to earn a living and how, being poor, he naturally spoke

71

French, the language of the poor, but English in his work, in order to 'get on'. In 1964 Gilles Groulx made his first full-length film, *Le Chat dans le Sac,* which today has become a classic of its kind. This film showed quite definitely that direct cinema, its techniques and its aesthetic ideas, in the hands of French teams had acquired a new meaning. It was no longer merely observing life in a humorous way but serving a cause that, in the years that followed, was to become the *raison d'être* of a whole group of intellectuals and artists, foremost among them the film-makers in the province of Quebec; to affirm the authenticity, the particularity and the originality of the French ethnic group in a bilingual country that was first dependent on France, then on Britain.

Le Chat dans le Sac carries on the revolution that can be seen in Godard's films as well as in those of the 'candid eye', concentrating on a precise goal – the awareness of being 'Quebecan'. The two young actors are mostly playing themselves, and keep their own christian names. Claude Godbout, an actor in search of identity, is Claude, a journalist in search of himself. Barbara Ulrich, the director's wife, a young English-speaking Jewess, is Barbara, an actress stranded in Montreal, in love with Claude and trying to make her way in the theatre. Claude broods over his own uselessness from morning till night and succumbs to his obsession with politics, so much so that Barbara, who wants to love and work and create, can no longer bear it. Although Barbara belongs to an ethnic minority, she has the confidence that only an English education can give, whereas Claude is completely lost in his efforts to find a national identity. Barbara talks of Brecht, Claude of Jean-Paul Sartre and Frantz Fanon. What is admirable about the film is its tone, a sort of monologue in two voices where the characters never cease to be introspective, and which passes from dialogue to monologue to commentaries 'off screen', or the other way round. *Le Chat dans le Sac* is composed like a poem and is what Godard has never been able to produce – a subjectively political film; also Groulx takes advantage of direct cinema to make the characters seem more intensely present and to intensify, too, the audience's participation in what happens to them. In its composition the film still shows signs of the classical cinema but Groulx is a master of both sound and image, sound – words, noises and

Alexis Tremblay and his wife Marie in Pierre Perrault's *Le Règne du Jour*

Pierre Perrault, right, with Alexis Tremblay, one of the characters in *Le Règne du Jour*

A scene from *Le Règne du Jour*

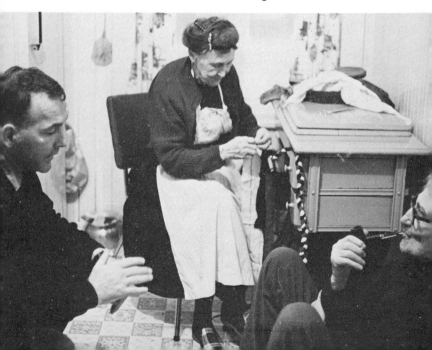

music – giving its tone to the image. In Groulx's second full-length film, *Ou ètes-vous donc?* (from the title of a pop song in Quebec), actors are placed in a situation that starts from a subject that involves them, and they elaborate the core of the film during the making of it while the director, keeping a strict check on the way work progresses, sees to its general development, which aims to show, once again, what Quebec is becoming.

The wheel has come full circle. French-speaking Canadians have used both the 'candid eye' and the 'New Wave' methods to their own advantage, and have created an original cinema in which, more intensely perhaps than in any other medium, they have set down the facts about French Canada.

But for a wholly new departure we must turn to Pierre Perrault. At first he had no avowed political aims but was seeking, through the intensity and complexity of his testimony, to go gradually back into history and to try to find the hidden origins of what had survived of France in Canada. This search produced three full-length films: *Pour la Suite du Monde* in 1963, *Le Règne du Jour* in 1967, and *Les Voitures d'Eau* in 1968.

The people shown in all these films live in the Ile-aux-Coudres, a small island in the St Lawrence about fifty miles upstream from Quebec where, until recently, at any rate when *Pour la Suite du Monde* was being made, a whole way of life that was quite outside the march of history still continued, at least among the old who lived entirely in the memory of the past when Jacques Cartier stayed on the island on September 6 and 7 1535 and gave it the name it still bears. At the time he made this film Pierre Perrault had, for over ten years, been familiar with Baie-Saint-Paul, on the north bank of the St Lawrence facing the island, and he was married to a local girl; he had known old Alexis Tremblay, the tutelary figure of the first two films, for a long time. A legend, he discovered, had survived about the fishing for porpoise (or more exactly, beluga) which had ended twenty-five years earlier, and in the islanders' memories this fishing had become magnified. Perrault asked them to recall it and made it the subject of his first full-length film, in which Michel Brault's contribution can be seen in the photography. It is often very fine in spite of the very free direction. In *Le Règne du Jour* Perrault, who this time was solely responsible for the direction, took old Alexis Tremblay, his

75

wife Marie, their son Leopold and their daughter-in-law on a journey to the country of their ancestors – western France, from whence the forebears of the present inhabitants of Quebec emigrated. When they got home, Perrault got the Tremblay family and their friends to talk about the journey and their discoveries. The remarkably good cutting is comparable with that of Resnais' early films, because Perrault, like Resnais, seems to rediscover old memories that are no longer individual but collective, the subsoil of past centuries. The rites celebrated at the death of a pig, the priest's appearance, are compared in France and in Canada. Suddenly the image Alexis has carved in his imagination of a France that is truly sublime at last comes to life in the person of Robert Martin, a game-keeper who describes how he was arrested and deported to Buchenwald, with a simplicity and a naturalness that take one's breath away. Very fast cutting mixes past, present and future, concentrating on feelings or on the continuity of ideas. To Perrault, each sentence spoken sends back to some wholly concrete experience. Man's imagination does not rise out of nothing, even if it seems to loom up out of an ancient darkness. Is it not burdened with the whole history of man?

In 1969 Perrault's third full-length film appeared. He had made it at the same time as he made *Le Règne du Jour*, and had worked on it for a long time before showing it publicly. This time we never leave Quebec, and the action all takes place on the Ile-aux-Coudres and the bank of the St Lawrence. From time immemorial the people on the island have built their own wooden boats, schooners or 'water-carriages', as they are called on the island, but these can no longer compete with the large metal ships chartered by the English companies. The islanders find that 'progress' comes to them just when they seem to be growing into an awareness that they no longer have the means to fight the other Canada on equal terms – that is, English Canada with its monopoly of wealth and of the means of production.

The narrative centres around two parts: one, the building of the last canoe – a sort of small-scale schooner – at the time when the film was made; the other, the departure from the island and the problems encountered in the outside world, particularly a dockers' strike at Trois-Rivières which once again emphasises the creaky way in which the social machine

Les Voitures d'Eau by
Pierre Perrault

grinds round. Yet the men who have built these ships are remarkable and have managed to survive terrible historical, economic and physical conditions through the mere strength of their hands. Perrault's technique is honed down to perfection; language remains pre-eminent, yet is closely linked with the living action. Everyone on the island, including the key characters of the first two films, the ancestral Alexis Tremblay, his son Leopold Tremblay, and Grand Louis the story-teller, all show an inexhaustible knowledge of the land and its people. Fast cutting, in which sentences run together, linked or balanced, emphasises the critical side of a careful, deeply involved description that centres on a new character, Laurent Tremblay, who owns a schooner but lacks the means to confront the modern world.

Perrault's progress is clear. *Les Voitures d'Eau* is in a sense the final part of a trilogy that began with *Pour la Suite du Monde* and *Le Règne du Jour*. Perrault is ready to admit that he has found direct cinema the most powerful method with which to catch life as it really is. But he is not content to catch life raw – he arranges it, edits it in every sense of the word, first of all through his detailed knowledge of the place, the characters and the situation he describes. He does not try to catch reality completely spontaneously or in a sort of primal innocence. The filming takes several months, sometimes a year or two, but it goes ahead at an irregular pace, sometimes even according to the demands of the cutting. The situation described in *Les Voitures d'Eau* is crystallised by three events: first, the building of the boat which brings to life not just a craft long practised on the island but all kinds of memories; second, the strike that keeps Laurent Tremblay, his team immobilised at Trois-Rivières purely by chance; third, the fire in an old unused schooner which shows the growing emotion on Laurent Tremblay's face and arouses other reflections and feelings; this scene was suggested by Bernard Gosselin, the cameraman. Obviously Perrault is in his own way creating a novel and has a deep knowledge of all the elements that form it; but he pushes these elements into real life and the finished product refers to this reality, to the growing awareness of a sense of community, which is ready to be merged with the French-Canadian or Quebecan community as a whole.

78

Un Pays sans bon Sens (1970) and *L'Acadie, l'Acadie* (1971), begun almost at the same time in 1968, show the start of a more radical attitude. Produced for the English section of the National Film Board of Canada, *Un Pays sans bon Sens* tries to describe an abstract idea, that of country. The film is divided into three quite distinct parts. The first – 'Sketch-book scenes' – introduces Didier Dufour, a geneticist doctor of science who returns to his village, Baie Saint-Paul, on the mainland facing the Ile-aux Coudres. The director soon shows us the sort of folklore that falsifies all values. In the second part – 'Rejecting the sketch-book' – a new character, Maurice Chaillot, graduate in literature from the Western Provinces, describes his experiences as a French Canadian who is ashamed of his origins because he grew up in a situation in which the French language is condemned to disappear and has no future. Then comes·the thesis (or if you prefer it, the hypothesis) on which the film is to be based: a sort of as yet unformed awareness in French Canadians, as Perrault sees them, that their country will henceforth be called Quebec, and that a country does exist in which they belong, in which they are at home. The third part – 'Return to the sketch-book' – gives a logical conclusion to a carefully considered analysis that arises out of what is shown of a particular place and particular characters; and none of it, Perrault insists, is there unnecessarily.

The film's political colour becomes obvious, not merely because René Levesque, leader of the newest party in the province of Quebec, appears in it now and then. Opposition is in fact much more deeply rooted in the hearts of individual people. In order to make his point more strongly Perrault not only confronts his two main characters, who through their background are intellectuals, with working-class people but builds up his theme in a threefold way. In the centre is French Canada and Quebec; upstream, if you like, is the example of the Indians, the memory of an almost vanished race which has been unable to adapt itself, yet which occupied the country before the arrival of the French and the English; downstream there is Brittany and the feelings of frustration of a province filled with history and yet unable to find its rightful place in the whole, which is called France.

Un Pays sans bon Sens (a paradoxical title that might be

L'Acadie, l'Acadie by Pierre Perrault and Michel Brault

translated as *It's a mad, mad, mad, mad country*) goes far beyond the detail of its own story and becomes a treatise on minorities, not so much because they express an anarchical protest, as because they are rooted in the past, in tradition. Pierre Perrault's last film made with Michel Brault, *L'Acadie, l'Acadie,* shows a period of revolt among students at the French-speaking university of Moncton in New Brunswick, previously Acadie, a province from which part of the population was expelled two hundred years ago. After the conquest of Canada by the British some of its people went to Louisiana, others returned to Brittany. The whole film takes place against this historical background; on the one hand, there is the memory of a not very distant past still alive in people's minds; on the other, there is Quebec, the neighbouring province, a burning example of a community that still holds the majority but seems condemned to be slowly absorbed.

The film starts from a very small incident. French-speaking students revolt to obtain payment of their fees and to make sure that they will not be handicapped in comparison with the all-powerful and much older neighbouring English-speaking university, U.N.B. (University of New Brunswick). There are three parts: first, a wave of strikes and demonstrations starting in 1968; then the vacation, the return home to the village life of what used to be Acadie; finally the second wave of strikes in 1969, the occupation of the science block, and expulsion by the police. The fight very soon turns on the defence of the students' French-speaking heritage. This awareness comes at a time of transition, when assimilation by the United States and English Canada is taking place increasingly fast yet French Canadians, though they no longer belong to the past, are not yet part of the American future in which all differences are supposed to be flattened out.

In a profound sense this is a political film, but it has no meaning except in relation to its young characters. For the first time Perrault breaks with the world of his elders or, more precisely, with that of the old. His eye becomes sharper, and concentrates on four people: two boys, Michel Blanchard, the younger, and Bernard Gauvin, the intellectual, and two girls, Blondine Maurice who wants to believe in the future and Irène Doiron who is haunted by the idea of suicide. In Perrault's now classic

F

81

manner the analysis is built up on discussions but this time there is a difference because these discussions are linked to an explosive situation, certainly not important compared with other more harshly suppressed revolts, yet fundamental because we can clearly see the nub of the problem, the reason for oppression.

Un Pays sans bon Sens and *L'Acadie, l'Acadie*, like all Perrault's work, suffer from having been made in French, which gives them a limited appeal among those who do not speak French. But with the smallest amount of effort and intelligence, it can perfectly well be sub-titled in English or in any other language, so long as the translator really understands the original and its spirit and has a complete mastery of both French and the language into which he is translating. This applies to all direct cinema films. Direct cinema, as it has been defined in this book, implies a passionate reaction against the cinema of excessive simplification, the kind I have been denouncing: a cinema where visual symbolism reigns triumphant and all is for the best in the best of all possible worlds, pigeon-holed into a few fundamental groups – French, English (and American), Soviet (or Russian) etc. Direct cinema demands really hard work from the audience, and finds its greatest response in its country of origin. It opens up the way, as the whole of Perrault's work has done, to new means of expression made possible by the use of light Video tape-recorders, using half-inch, extremely manageable tape on which real montage can now be achieved. Perhaps it is *his own truth* that Perrault shows us, but in order to do so he goes back to the living sources of a particular society where language was born and the behaviour of people laid down.

In other words, Perrault set off one day to discover his country, as he puts it in an admirable text he wrote in answer to questions from Guy Gauthier which appeared in *Image et Son* in April 1965: 'I have got inside people's homes. I have got hold of their past. Nothing is more real than an old man telling of an event he has lived through. Often the facts themselves may not have any value but the telling of them has. I keep quiet. I listen.' And suddenly the sense of history shows itself. Perrault is quite unlike Lévi-Strauss who, through an interpreter and at a distance, collects the facts brought to light by an inquiry among the Brazilian Indians; he starts from an immediate contact and, if he can, makes two people talk to each other until they forget him. '. . . a living dialogue must be drawn from the very substance of the people, and this is possible only when they are able to stand up against each other, or else against a third party. In other words, yeast is needed. And it means having lived with them for a long time as well.' Perrault's aim is 'to trigger off a certain action (living, livable, possible, wished, longed for by the actors in spite of the camera) . . . to make events produce themselves before me – and not for me'. Perrault starts with the convention of performance in order to multiply it by the whole connected force of the action provoked and the imaginations of the people involved in it. Far from wanting to strip reality, as Leacock does, he exalts it, recreating it in order to transfigure it. An ideal mixture of Leacock's method, which is purely cinematic, and Perrault's, which is more poetic and more literary, in which the 'living' – which is more or less spontaneous and more or less organised – and the 'lived' – with its historical structure, its sense of becoming – will one day produce an autonomous cinema that has finally broken completely with established methods of expression; but this is still only a dream.

Finally, I must mention a recent work by the producer of *Pour la Suite du Monde*, Fernand Dansereau who, in search of an original method of sociological cinema, took 30,000 metres of film that was finally condensed into two hours to become *Saint-Jérôme*, about a small town of 35,000 inhabitants thirty miles from Montreal. The people there saw the rushes as they appeared, discussed them, made suggestions, and had the right to censor what they did not approve of. A friendly atmosphere was established. The final cutting, in spite of a wish for objectivity, was not done until Dansereau had made his own choice and expressed his own vision of the enormous amount of material collected. The definitive version was agreed by those involved and the film was shown outside the ordinary circuit in local cinemas. After its projection in order to illustrate a point raised by a member of the audience a fragment which did not appear in the final film was shown, called 'satellite film'. *Saint-Jérôme* helped exchanges of opinion among the people there when the film was being made and, when it was shown, produced another kind of participation. In his next film, Fernand Dansereau is going even further: 'It is a film made by the people of the south and centre of Montreal. It will be a story this time and will last an hour and a half . . . In it, I am no longer a film-maker, in a way. It is the people themselves who are making the film . . . Perrault has gone before us . . . He started by bringing people to mythology; for my part, I begin from the everyday. It is not necessarily contradictory.'

Dansereau's efforts at founding a social cinema are not unlike those of the English-Canadian Colin Low since 1967, in the series *Challenge for Change*, the first and most famous example of which was called *Newfoundland Project*, a series of short films lasting from fifteen to twenty minutes, made on location and closely involving local people who expressed themselves as individuals especially concerned with this or that problem. In the end the reaction of the whole community is filmed or, more generally, the film is shown in public with a discussion, which is a vital element in work of the kind. Sociological experience obviously takes on a poetic or political slant:

'The "Fogo Island Project" (the original title of the enterprise) was designed to investigate the reactions of the community when its people and its problems were filmed in depth and the result was played back to them for discussion and criticism . . . Our approach was to involve the entire community in the process of self-analysis and problem solving. This approach affected the way we made the films and also the way they were shown. At all stages the emphasis was to involve the community in the decisions to be made. The people selected the topics and they were involved in editing decisions when the films were played back. They also determined the extent of the distribution of the film, if in fact they decided it should be seen by others.'

Canada is the cradle of direct cinema, and some very individual films using lightweight cameras have come out of Toronto. Allan King, who started in documentary and television, in 1967 showed *Warrendale*, a film about a very special school for the re-education of psychotic children, and in 1970 *A Married Couple* in which, with their agreement, he followed a couple's life for some time. In this, although Allan King failed to realise it, we return to the voyeurism that belongs to the classic tradition of cinema, and stay on a level of what is trivial and accidental. The first two films of a one-time design engineer, Morley Markson, are subtler: *The Diary of Zero the Fool* (1969) and *Breathing Together: Revolution of the. Electric Family* (1970) integrate this idea of voyeurism in the films from the start. Indeed, it is the subject of the first film, the story of a half-crazy voyeur who in real life committed suicide a little later, while *Breathing Together* – which mixes the stars of the 'alternative' America, Jerry Rubin, Abbie Hoffman, Andrew Sinclair, Allen Ginsberg, the Black Panthers, as well as Buckminster Fuller, inventor of the geodesic domes – gives a very personal synthesis and suggests a romantic, rootless future, light years from the world of Pierre Perrault, who is equally Canadian. Morley Markson, using a nervous form of cutting, expresses the movement of his own sensibility through the remarks of other people, and, in a way, renews the old *cinéma d'auteur*; but he does not analyse the problem in depth.

Jean Rouch

Although film libraries now contain any number of mono-graphs on Antonioni, Bergman and Hitchcock – all of them great creators according to recognised standards – they contain very little on the work of Leacock, Perrault and Jean Rouch. It is hardly surprising that Leacock, the most radically new of them, is still unknown; and the fact that Perrault is only just beginning to emerge from anonymity – and that only in French-speaking countries – can be explained. But that Jean Rouch, who is known all over the world, and who would seem to be the most popular of them, is ignored by critics and experts only proves that where the cinema is concerned everything still needs to be done. Antonioni, Bergman and Hitchcock are story-tellers *par excellence*, at best they 'illustrate' an earlier text, conceived within the limitations of fiction, either from a novel (Hitchcock) or from theatre (Bergman); in other words, a text which is heir to several centuries of the theatre and the novel. Antonioni, who is more 'modern' and more closely in touch with abstract contemporary art, attempts to find sculptural and musical analogies that forecast some of the efforts of the American undergound; but he never really frees himself from tradition. Leacock, Perrault and Rouch, on the other hand, base their work on purely cinematic premises and cast aside the whole heritage that has come straight down from D. W. Griffith, the first creator of forms in the cinema.

The only thing that links Leacock, Perrault and Rouch is, I think, their common admiration for Robert Flaherty, and above all for the Flaherty of *Nanook*. After this their paths divide. I should like to define Leacock as the technician of 'new cinema', the anti-Hitchcock, because of his categorical rejection of the old cinematographic 'grammar', the super-professional believer in free direction who follows none of the text-book rules; and Perrault as the ideological thinker of this same 'new cinema', the anti-Antonioni because of his refusal to crush his characters under a kind of existential destiny, the super-professional of free performance whose rules are not to be found in any manual for script-writers. As for Jean Rouch, who seeks to be the author, in the narrative sense, of his films, and who in several cases has been his own cameraman, it is hard to know how to classify him. He came to the cinema as an amateur, having bought a small Bell and Howell camera in 1946 in the flea-market, and during a journey to Niger discovered all kinds of things that were impossible to set down in mere writing, in a notebook or in a still photograph. He showed some friends the film he had brought back on a hippopotamus chase and was advised to keep his camera on a tripod in future to get a prettier picture. Our hero gave as good as he got, mocked his academic advisers who defended the 'beautiful' documentary and went his own way, even anticipating several of the objectives of the new American cinema or underground, which Jonas Mekas was to celebrate after 1959.

Jean Rouch admits freely that to him the cinema is a hobby, an essential pastime that takes up more and more of his time, alongside his activities as an ethnographer. As secretary of the Ethnographic Films Committee at the Musée de l'Homme he has never stopped trying to make his colleagues accept the basic importance of the cinema in taking down raw reality, sound and image being inseparable, and thus keeping track of events which until now we have know only in a fragmentary way, either through the image alone, either still or moving, or else by language alone. He likes to give the example of the stone drums in the Dogon country, 'which for centuries have no doubt been played at the funerals of men whose skeletons are found even today hidden in nearby shelters'.[1] The small goatherds used to practise these rhythms quite spontaneously by tapping the worn stone with pebbles; today, these rhythms are played only on skin drums belonging to the elders. The children go to school and no longer have time to practise, so a tradition is about to be lost; perhaps the synchronised camera can catch these ancestral rhythms for the last time, rhythms linked to an exactly known mythology and transmitted exactly as they have been for centuries.

The ethnographic cinema raises many problems that cannot be discussed in this short study; here, we can only suggest possible views of the ethnographic cinema and, through it, of the work of Jean Rouch in the cinema. In an article in the *Revue Française de Sociologie* (April–June 1967) Colette Piault of the French National Centre for Scientific Research, while suggesting the possibilities opened up to sociologists and ethnologists by the synchronised cinema, emphasised the material difficulties and the near-impossibility of filming long scenes continuously, and refused to see a panacea in it: 'Nothing can replace (for the sociologist-ethnologist) the reflection and the elaboration of hypotheses later verified with the help of the right instruments . . . Not to disturb the place we are working in, not to be slaves of technical necessities, really to know what we are filming, and to know why we are filming – these are the rules we must respect.' A little earlier, in the same article, Colette Piault deplores the fact that synchronised editing does not give the same freedom as classic editing, in which the sounds are 'selected'. One may wish, as she does, that the material used were surer and more manageable; but the revolution, if it can be called that, seems irreversible. Perhaps prudent critics like this will allow us to guess what we may expect when images can be registered magnetically, when they are as easy to efface as sound, and as easy to

---

[1] Extract from the preface to the *First Selective International Catalogue of Ethnographic Films on Black Africa*, published by Unesco in 1967.

control without waiting for their development in the laboratory. We are about to enter not merely the age of the image, foreseen by the prophets of the silent era, but an age in which reality will be analysed not through distant feelings recorded on canvas or paper but taken down in the very same moment, when there is the immediate contact that alters everything, for 'author' as well as 'reader'. The revolution of the modern media, which Marshall McLuhan loves to talk about, can already be seen in this tool which is still at a crude stage yet will continue to be refined until our bookish view of the world is changed into a cinematic view of it. Theses will be written on James Joyce[1] and the foretaste of direct cinema to be found in *Ulysses* and *Finnegan's Wake*. *Ulysses*, starting from a classical idea of cinematic cutting, introduced the monologue and the verbal continuum and *Finnegan's Wake*, becoming a pure phonetic amalgam, showed the destruction of narrative in favour of hearing. Joyce himself gave an amazing reading from the book, and suddenly *Finnegan's Wake* can be seen as revolutionary, tolling the knell of writing, on which we still live.

Jean Rouch's great quality, in spite of his many fields of activity, is this realisation that the cinema is taking us somewhere else and that, in it, everything is allowed. His limitation is that he does not commit himself completely enough to ratify his intuitions through contact with living reality. Leacock and Perrault use words and sentences objectively, although in very different ways; Rouch, however, uses them as a means of escape, a kind of fleeing forward, or rather backwards. In terms of a collective unconscious that should make African film-makers criticise him harshly, Rouch rejects history, believes in nothing but individual drama, anecdote, detail isolated from its context. In this way, and in his fiction films particularly, he can perhaps be considered as the finished representative of the 'art of provocation' that Jean-Luc Godard has inherited from .him, the mechanics of which Rouch himself has described admirably in a number of interviews.

In the first (*Cahiers du Cinéma* No. 144, June 1963) he

[1] Jay Leyda, well known for his work on Eisenstein, is now trying to discover which films seen by Joyce can be traced in his work.

explained what he had done in *La Punition*, which he had just finished cutting. The film, which was made in about two days, describes various meetings between a schoolgirl, Nadine, and a young man in the Luxembourg Gardens, then between her and a man in his forties who asks her to his house. The young people either have nothing to say to each other or else emerge from their shyness to provoke each other. Once again we find the idea of time used as it was in *Chelsea Girls*, as I described it at the end of the section on Richard Leacock. 'When I was filming I realised something very important,' said Rouch, 'the interest which the tiredness of actors and technicians gives the film. The part I like best in *La Punition* is the part we made as late as possible, the scene with the engineer, when we were all exhausted . . . Nadine was flat out, and so she had no reflexes.' And, he went on a little later: 'People, perhaps because there's a camera there, create something quite different and create it spontaneously.' Here, I think, lies the secret of all Rouch's work – his Parisian films like *Chronique d'un Été*, *La Punition*, or *Gare du Nord*, a Franco-African film like *La Pyramide Humaine*, or purely African films like *Les Maîtres Fous* or *Jaguar*. Language, presented as in *Gare du Nord*, written in advance, or improvised as in nearly all the other films, sometimes hung onto the action, in direct cinema, or else looking back on it in the form of a commentary yet still in direct cinema, takes its meaning from this tension and this weariness.

The criticisms that one could make of Rouch's method have already been expressed by Leacock and Perrault when they defined the character of their own work.

'With Rouch,' said Leacock (*Cahiers du Cinéma* No. 140, February 1963) '– I've seen his *Chronique d'un Été* and *Les Maîtres Fous* – it seems to me that, although his films are so interesting, the most important thing that has ever happened to the people he chooses to film is the fact that he has filmed them.' And Perrault adds: 'Rouch's characters are prone to introspection rather than action . . . they are reflections of themselves.' (*Image et Son*, interview already quoted.) These remarks do not apply in the least to films like *Jaguar* or *La Chasse au Lion à l'Arc*, but they emphasise the second movement in Rouch's work; after the provocation comes the reaction, the liking for explanation and narrative in the most literal sense of

89

Jean Rouch's *Petit à Petit*

the word. There is talk and storytelling, often a very long way from the reality of things and of beings. Once again there is reason to remember Jean-Luc Godard, with whom Rouch has a good deal in common. The film, a mixture of truth and fiction, is directed in a way that runs more or less counter to the characters, or against them, in order to make some of Rouch's obsessions clear. Today *Jaguar* exists in a definitive 35mm version, with an offscreen commentary by the three men who made the journey from Niger to Ghana. One day in 1958 when he was sitting in the front row of the Cinémathèque Française in the Rue d'Ulm Jean Rouch made a commentary into a microphone in the darkness on the complete three-hour silent version, sometimes describing the action, sometimes miming the characters' behaviour through words. This is probably Rouch's most personal, most complete film, swept along by his fervour, and suddenly lighting up his whole adventurous treatment of the cinema, his search for myths through the film; and yet, although made in 1953, it has still not been publicly screened. Having gone far beyond all truth, Rouch first of all tells us his stories.

Rouch marks the transition between Jean Renoir and Georges Rouquier on the one hand, and Godard and Chris Marker on the other, and represents a very French tradition of direct cinema. All Renoir's films were made with synchronised sound, often in an atmosphere of improvisation that means they have resisted the ravages of time far better than Marcel Carné's have. In the whole history of the classical cinema they have remained the most modern, already foreshadowing the work of Richard Leacock, in which the director is his own cameraman.

Georges Rouquier is thought by Perrault to be the immediate precursor of his 'lived cinema', and *Farrebique* the French cousin of *Pour la Suite du Monde*, but *Farrebique* was made in 1946 with the huge cameras that made any freedom of movement impossible. Rouquier had no chance of continuing his work in this direction, except perhaps in *Lourdes et ses Miracles* (1963). He is the first victim of our production system.

Chris Marker, a great traveller and a champion of militant cinema, first showed his own very personal, almost precious vision of the social contradictions existing around the world (*Cuba, Sí* and *Le Joli Mai*).

Mario Ruspoli deserves a place of his own for his *Inconnus de la Terre* (1962), which shows the wretched life of the peasants of la Lozere, filmed by Michel Brault, and more recently for his presentation of a psycho-drama, *Le Vif Mariage,* animated by Dr Pierre Bour.

In his first French film, *Les Enfants de Néant* (1968), Michel Brault, merely by using his own techniques, showed the kind of spontaneous France that had never been seen on the screen, in which facts and people spoke for themselves without any preconceived subjective or sociological modifications. The film's subject is the fate of a Breton peasant forced to leave his land.

The Small Screen[1]

Is direct cinema a technical process? By definition it would seem that television belongs to the same world as direct cinema. It is a new means of telecommunication which, through the analysis, reconstitution and electrical transmission of images by a modulation of frequency, shows the audience the event taking place 'directly'. Thus television moves ahead of the previously made film.

In this first sense of the word – its technical meaning – direct cinema means: without material interference, immediate, without intermediary. By extension, one would call 'direct' the transmission, at a pre-arranged date, of what is caught by direct cinema.

This technique gives the audience the chance of being contemporary with the event, of having a realistic point of view ('it's like being there') and thus feeling suspense in relation to what is about to happen: suspense not in relation to fiction but in relation to the reality of what is happening in the world. In this sense, as has been said, television is 'the machine for registering the future' (J. C. Bringuier), the means by which the future, caught at the very moment in which it is realised, is transmitted directly to the audience. This produces the magic of a medium that *almost* allows us to work on the future in

[1] This section is by Nicole Rouzet-Albagli.

order to turn it into the present, that makes possible this kind of swing in time, the present revealed being the past in relation to what the television is *still* about to show, encroaching ceaselessly on the future, as if it had no past. Yet the spectator is by no means contemporary with this action that is making the future come to pass. Although the fact that he is watching in a way justifies what is shown to him and makes it come about, his spontaneity is still quite passive; because he is outside the work being done by the camera, just the short distance away that separates the catching of the event from its transmission; we, the viewers, see the image exactly as it becomes past instead of present, hustled off by what is to follow. The camera may make the future out of the present but we, the viewers, make the present into the past. Or, more precisely, we are present at the actual unrolling of history, but *we are not contemporary* with the work carried out by the camera. In this way we learn that we are *merely* the viewers of what is happening, and that the only field of action offered to us is to be present at something that is taking place elsewhere.

This view that supports, yet is quite outside, what is happening, is found in the cinema as well. But in that case there is a special building, there is the audience's attention, and the whole social function of the film which is projected just because there is an audience. The film starts at a fixed hour, and is preceded by an interval during which the crowd, which is anything but 'solitary', may move about. Television belongs to private life. There is nothing festive about it because the spectacle is not put on for our benefit. The images are shown to other people before we switch on: television time is any time. This means that what we are shown has nothing odd about it, it is taken as coming from everyday life. A documentary that is unbearable in the cinema may be seen on television: our attention is naturalistic. In this sense television is the poor relation of the cinema; one forgets the medium for the message and our set has no existence till the moment one turns the switch. The cameraman is the man who first turns the switch onto life.

But realism of outlook, and eyes looking directly at events, imply a limitation of the field of vision: the frame contains only a part of reality. And it is harder to shift a camera than to turn one's head. Television seeks to multiply the points of view by

93

putting a number of cameras in a number of privileged positions. Ideally, the spectacle seen is at the point where the eyes of all kinds of viewers converge – all possible viewers, in fact. Plenty of progress has been made since women announcers had purple hair, the same broadcast was put out twice for viewers on 441 and 809 lines, and when it was a feast to be able to show the coronation of Queen Elizabeth from start to finish. The camera's eyesight is perfect; it sees everything at once and knows everything. To the cameraman, all is transparent. So a whole aesthetic of objectivity is developed – for technical reasons, in part – because in fact, as Jean-Claude Bringuier says, 'from the technical point of view, direct cinema does not mean spontaneity'. Nothing takes more preparation than the setting up of heavy, complicated, unwieldy cameras, and managing to film at all is sometimes such a *tour de force* that merely to succeed in doing so is the object of the broadcast. On the other hand, direct cinema, as well as being a technical process, implies that the camera should be as self-effacing as possible. What it wants to show the audience is the event itself, quite independently of the eye that is watching it. People forget, however, or like to forget, that there is never a 'universal' point of view that does not become schematic, indifferent and abstract. The universal point of view is that of Everyman, that is, the viewer who is taught and told with every broadcast that he has no influence on things, that he is not responsible for what he sees, because only the event counts, in the sense in which it is presented to him.

There is a mystique in technique, a mystique in objectivity, and this is the double danger that lies in wait for a 'direct' television broadcast. Nothing deliberate is involved but technical possibilities and the maker's intentions may intervene. True direct cinema, on the other hand, direct cinema as a style, is born from a struggle against the technical procedure known as 'direct'.

The lightweight camera with its synchronised sound. Technical discoveries give rise to another demand. It might be said that they show a new way of reading reality; but it is only by approaching it indirectly that its makers will be able to achieve the ideal direct cinema. They will use lighter cameras that can

94

glide everywhere and get about unnoticed. This is what Mario Ruspoli says on the subject (*Le Groupe synchrone cinématographique léger*. Unesco, 1963) 'The "small screen" used the 16mm image from the start, an image so far used only by amateurs and infinitely less expensive than the classic film of 35mm cinema. Thus, from one day to the next, the 16mm format found a huge international outlet.'

Direct cinema as a new style of approaching the world began, then, with television and it is from television that this new aesthetic idea will spread and gradually take over the cinema; being ten years ahead of it, it is going to transform the documentary profoundly.

Learning to look and listen. All cameramen seriously interested in this new way of looking at reality agree that the mere technical procedure involved is fascinating. The fact of using a lightweight camera demands and allows more than television filming does. In the infatuation with lightweight cameras over the past ten years, there has been the frightful danger that as things can be filmed, they *are* filmed. 'The technical possibilities open to one in the cinema are a snare,' says Bringuier. It is not enough to film people and things in direct cinema because they are filmable, it is not enough to show them because they are interesting.

This is saying that direct cinema is the opposite of simple immediacy: it brings in the intermediary factors that exist in every true approach to knowledge. It is the opposite of *cinéma vérité* which seeks to behave as if the camera did not exist: indeed, it tries to give the camera a hypnotic sense of both presence and absence, making it a tool that mediates between the cameraman and the world, and holds the delicate balance which he establishes between interpretation and objectivity, between his *participation* in the event and the way in which he *allows* it to appear. Far from trying to give us a perfect equivalent of reality direct cinema shows that, in the real world, we have forgotten how to look and listen. We pass over things, we use people, we look beyond them or we project our own problems and our own desires on to them. It teaches us, once again, the kind of rigorous, open observation which, through its very existence, fights and improves the increasingly poor fiction that

95

the mass media put out daily to build up our personal mythology.

The school of direct cinema has as many styles as it has filmmakers. But it is still possible to find some things that are constant in it.

Belonging to the milieu. The lightweight camera makes it possible to follow the life of a town or a person, or to follow something that happens. As a rule the team lives on the spot for a fairly long time in order to become integrated into the world it seeks to describe. André Gazut, a cameraman in Swiss television, finds that it is essential not only to get beyond the stage at which the team and its equipment appear unusual, but to wait until people have found their right balance in relation to the new element. When someone says 'You still there?' you can start filming. In Gazut's short film *Le Médecin de Campagne*, the doctor's authority and presence are used instead of this familiarity; in a way he was standing surety for the intruders, acting as mediator between the village and the director.

Jacques Krier, of French television, feels that the cameraman is integrated into the milieu as soon as he is regarded as a worker. But, at the same time, he must also take on the function of 'outsideness', strangeness, because this allows people to say more than they would among themselves, in their own families; inside their own homes they start talking and tell him what is not mentioned in ordinary life. The camera's intrusion must be interpreted as a sociological event which makes the group live in a new way. It will depend on the cameraman, on the sort of relationship he can establish, whether this new experience is fruitful and liberating or whether, on the contrary, it is alienating. 'One is a guest, one replaces the evening storyteller.'

Hubert Knapp and Jean-Claude Bringuier consider that the essential thing is to find the right tone, but they too have to start by seeking a place or people which, in a sense, they already bear within themselves. The friendly relationship that is established comes from the encounter between these special, mythical places and people, and the reality that the film-maker discovers about them. The richness and surprisingness of what is discovered meets the inner world of each person involved,

96

film-maker and audience, and the film's life comes from the way the two worlds adjust to each other. In the series *Croquis* this discovery of reality is expressed through the theme of return: a deliberate return, as in the 'croquis' (sketches) of the town of Sète, or in the narrative, as when the camerman, André Labarthe, returns to his home town of Terrasson. (It might perhaps be compared with the return of old Alexis Tremblay to France, the land of his ancestors.) Return, as Bringuier says, 'to the unity between the real world and the golden age that is in us – insofar', he adds, 'as we seek it without patronage or smugness.'

Images and reality. Although it avoids the evasions of fiction, direct cinema fundamentally questions what the image is. First of all the image must indicate the real or, to use Christian Metz's analysis,[1] it must indicate reality enough for the audience 'to catch it in a realising way'.

But is what he is going to 'realise' the realistic reality that direct cinema quite rightly teaches him to go beyond? On the other hand, can one really go beyond this realistic realisation? 'The images one uses,' says Bringuier, 'are always pictorial.' He continues:

'The images in the present context carry their own alienation. Finally, the more a human group is really meaningful, that is, the stronger its complicity in what is happening, the less pictorial the images, and the more they are shot through by this understanding, the less they are transparent themselves; the more this meaning is discovered through the contradictions of society the more the images float about and the more the meaning is to be found behind them. Every broadcast implies an understanding of the social body . . . But one must know what the image is. Actually, it doesn't exist . . . The image, in a film, is a shot. The continuity of reality has no meaning in itself, because it is caught among other images, propelled, raised up, dragged away from itself to become part of the whole, which is moving. The image is

[1] See 'L'Impression de réalité', *Essais sur la signification au cinéma*, p. 16.

G

what it is, you cannot say what you are talking about when you talk of an image.

'. . . I think that art is "reactionary", that it carries its own contradiction within itself. Potentially *Potemkin* is always ahead of any of the revolutionary ideas you may read into it. The secret of art lies in betrayal. There is a subversive side to art. Art must be reactionary. Art resists . . .

'What I think is that I probably try, in making television films, to imitate the theoretical movement I have described here. But each film-maker tries to imitate this theoretical development in his own way.'

Cutting, direction. Can this contradiction in indirect direct cinema be resolved by the technique used? The question asks how much reconstruction is implied in the cutting. In order to clarify the problem, here are some extracts from a second interview with Jean-Claude Bringuier.

INTERVIEWER: '*I must admit that at first I was shocked when I heard you discussing cutting after the film's projection. Maybe my idea of direction was too romantic, but the amount of change that took place, although done constructively, scared me, because it seemed like trickery. Have you never found yourself faced with two or three possibilities in the cutting, all of them equally valid?*'

BRINGUIER: 'Ideally direction is not done in the cutting room. It depends what life turns up while you're filming, even with a particular theme running through it. All the time you're nudged by what reality brings you. You decide to give way to it or not up to a point, sometimes for quite ordinary reasons like time, money and available film. That little old woman or that landscape that seemed indispensable or brilliant may turn out to be completely stupid when you come to project what you've shot. The cutting stage is very different from the shooting.

'And there's another thing you should know: when you're making a film you're paralysed by the weather. But in a commercial film, if you've got to film on a sunny day at Deauville, you go to Deauville and wait for the sun. In television, credit's limited. If it isn't fine you've got to film just the same. This produces a rather strange effect, and you allow yourself to be guided by whatever turns up. This means you have to reconstruct. There is, in fact, a lack of determinism between one sequence and the next. There isn't just a single right way of cutting, there are several.

'In the film *Laurin*, for instance, the problem was very complex: the dramatic construction of *Laurin* had contradictory relationships with the personal time in Laurin's story. This meant that we needed a style like Faulkner's, going backwards not in flashbacks but by allowing what used to be to erupt into the narrative. The time-sequence of Laurin's life ran counter to the dramatic flow of the broadcast – strong times, weak times – and you've got to keep to the broadcast, which includes a dramatic value inherent in the projection itself.

'When you get down to it, you make an hour or half-hour film out of ten or fifteen hours' projection.

'. . . It's both embarrassing and fascinating. You've got to extract the nuggets from it. It's difficult, but it gives you freedom: you behave towards the reality you've collected as you do towards the original reality. A tiny bit closer: once you've sketched out the montage, once the form of the film has appeared, you see what's missing, what you never even thought of filming. Then you go back to fill in the gaps, and give yourself orders, sometimes very stern ones.

'. . . Do you know what the ideal film would be, for me? It would be a film where there was a single element, in the sense that there's water, air, and so on. Or rather, a film where you'd have a single climate as element. For instance, in *Terrasson*, there's that moment when André's alone; it's night-time, the neon lights are on behind him, the wind's blowing, he's going to cross a road that divides us from him and he's lit up violently by the headlamps of the passing cars. There are moments of light and moments of wind. I'd have liked the whole film to have stopped, in a static, contemplative way, at that sequence, which was probably quite insignificant to most people.'

All this makes me think that Christian Metz is both right and wrong then he speaks of the audience's 'realising intention'. He is right, because what the spectator is doing is in fact exactly what he is constantly not allowed to do in his life: he is making reality. But the realistic, non-realising attitude, which is his fate in everyday life, refuses to allow him to do this.

Socialism in Direct Cinema

Quite naturally direct cinema found itself most at home in the socialist countries, in the period when people wished to look squarely at reality without the embellishments customary in the 'cult of personality' period. The fact that the film industry was nationalised in these countries ought to have facilitated this spreading of direct cinema ideas. Very early on Richard Leacock, D. A. Pennebaker and Albert Maysles were welcomed with open arms in Moscow, Prague and East Berlin. The equipment used in these countries was not always the best, but the principle remained that films must be made on location, and people listened to when they expressed criticisms; that things must be shown 'as they really are' (Brecht), and this was true of fiction. Films made in Hungary and Czechoslovakia should be analysed carefully from this point of view.

Hungary went furthest of all in this search for frankness, and produced not so much direct cinema, as the only *cinéma-vérité* worthy of the name. In a careful report written for Unesco on the occasion of the round table conference held in Moscow from July 13–15 1965, Andras Kovacs analysed in detail the progress of direct cinema in Hungary, both in the cinema and in television, and its place in Hungarian life. He himself gave an example of it in 1964 when he made the frankest and most 'direct' film made in a socialist country, *The Unruly Ones* (*Nehéz emberek*). Kovacs quite simply went to see five very individual people who had suffered from bureaucratic rigidity, in their homes. A highly qualified workman had invented a new technique of folding steel plates, but although it was patented and used abroad his invention had had no success in Hungary. In a rudimentary workshop on a farm an engineer had made a tool that revolutionised work techniques: once again, only foreigners had been interested in it. Another engineer had invented a factory machine that was also exported abroad but for which he had received no reward; he consoled himself for it by playing the organ in church. And so on. Kovacs found inspiration in a *genre* that was very fashionable in Hungary in the early thirties – literary sociography – a *genre* that was to be extremely important in forming opinion among progressive intellectuals. 'The discovery of Hungary' was the title of the series on which novelist and poets as well as journalists worked and which even today, although they were not attempting to be lasting works, are the most authentic, the most moving testimony of the period that exists ... In Hungary, this kind of report on living reality, taking no account of literary standards and cutting out all divisions between novels, memoirs and scientific analyses, has tradition behind it.

In 1963 Andras Kovacs attended the MIPE-TV at Lyons, mentioned at the beginning of this book, and went home from it profoundly impressed by the new possibilities offered by 'spontaneous' cinema. He had already made two full-length films according to the usual fictional techniques and a third was in preparation; and on his return to Budapest he had no idea of profiting from the experience he had gained at Lyons. While he was away a discussion had begun in Hungary on the career possibilities in the country, and a filmed inquiry on conditions of life and work among young engineers had been planned. As soon as it was formulated the idea was quashed. The subject seemed too delicate, and those who had considered it later thought – mistakenly – that it could not be treated with complete sincerity. As they said themselves: 'Either we could make it authentic, in which case it would not be allowed to be shown in public, or else we could make it in a way that meant it would get permission, in which case it wouldn't be worth making.' After his return to Hungary Kovacs heard of this idea and decided to use it. Deliberately he chose to make the film with interviews.

'To surprise people, to film them unexpectedly, would have been quite impossible because I had to choose my models (five men who were standing up to their negative surroundings and doing all they could to put their ideas into practice); they had to be ready, not just to collaborate themselves and to answer my questions, but to accept the risks which the discussion of their case and conflicts involved. I must

101

emphasise these risks, because what these men were giving to the whole world wasn't a mere transistory feeling, or a moral or even a political opinion; it was the essential element of their lives – their work – often the result of ten or fifteen years' labour, the success or failure of which could bring a fundamental change into their lives and that of their families. After all I've just said, could spontaneity come into it at all? Yes, within certain limitations, it could.'

Shooting in 35mm, you couldn't shatter the conventions that belonged to each one of these men. First of all, even today, there is no way of following characters through their daily lives in synchronised 35mm. Thus the director in a way begins with a working hypothesis: I've got involved with individuals and must accept them as they are. All through the film each of the five characters explains himself in a single take, except the man who invented the factory machine and plays the organ in church in the evenings. So it isn't a matter of considering, as Leacock suggests one should, what goes between the time the judge leaves his home and the time he arrives in court, when the plain father of a family turns into a judge. I have been able to see for myself the way this process may simplify things. Thanks to Kovacs, I met one of his main characters, the farming engineer who was in charge of a large agricultural organisation. This precise, exuberant man seemed more American than European. Efficiency was the thing he cared about, and he had nothing but sarcasm for a classic film by Karoly Makk – *The Obsessed,* I think it was. 'There were plenty of fine images,' he said, 'and in the end all the difficulties were solved in a miraculous kind of way.' (A shot of this film exists in *The Unruly Ones,* used in the same spirit.) But Karoly Makk is a sincere man and a talented artist. *The Unruly Ones* poses the problem of a truthful cinema twice over, first by its actual existence, then, more directly, by mentioning this earlier film which was very good in a traditional way; yet this does not prevent me regretting the relative limitations of Kovacs' film, which is taken from what its five heroes said in 'official' discussions, even when they were in revolt against 'official' routine. If Kovacs had gone deeper into his subject *The Unruly Ones* would have become more than a dialectical discussion and,

102

moving to a new level of sociological analysis, in the same struggle to establish the rights of ideas, would have denounced what was wrong even more radically than it did and have shown these remarkable men in full dimension, in both their public and private life.

Kovacs' method deserves consideration, however, no less than Pierre Perrault's, because of its extreme coherence. In the Unesco publication mentioned earlier Kovacs puts over his own point of view on the subject very revealingly:

'In the first part of the interview I questioned my characters on the professional problems which I knew they cared about. As a rule their replies were just tape-recorded, but we pretended to be filming as well. This helped to make them familiar with the camera and with the members of our team, and to slacken the tension they felt at the thought of having to face a filmed interview, a tension that lasted several days. As they had not been told what questions I was going to ask them they had prepared a number of answers of a professional kind, because of course we'd had to warn them that we'd be asking about their inventions. Once they'd given us these prepared answers (the vanity of showing oneself in the most favourable light is common to us all), they became calm and relaxed and, without being weighed down by responsibility, quite happily answered questions of a more personal kind that didn't strike them as very important, but which I felt were more important. One of the engineers, who had excellent ideas on the technical level, at the same time played a church organ, not just for his own pleasure but because it brought him in a little money as well. Another of his pastimes was learning languages. He knew seven, including Arabic, which he had begun to study because he had heard that Arab women were experts in love-making and he wanted – if he ever happened to meet one – to be able to talk to her without an interpreter. These small facts of course have no direct relationship with the professional or human qualities of the man interviewed, but they do help to complete the portrait and to give light and shade to the character.

'As the questions I asked were improvised I didn't know what sort of answers I would get. Often they took me by

103

LIVING CINEMA

surprise, and made me change the questions I had meant to ask later on (I did all the interviewing myself), which meant that the personality of the reporter was also revealed a little, as he often had to react spontaneously to the answers.

'As a rule it isn't hard to get a spontaneous reply from strangers, people questioned suddenly in the street or elsewhere, but the replies you get in such a way are usually rather dull. But in our case it was a case of asking economic or technical questions in a way that would give them tension and human interest. When I began, I wondered if my film wouldn't be too full of intellectual elements. I was afraid that the large amount of text and the close-up faces would be not just tiresome but actually unbearable to watch. I tried to bring some movement into it, to make my people move about and to give the camera greater possibilities. But after my first efforts at this kind of thing I stopped; I soon had to give up being cinematographic . . . The result was a curious film "very much a film in spite of its lack of cinematographic elements", as someone who had seen it wrote to me. Some people received it very favourably, delighted not to find the accessories and arrangements they knew all too well.'

Andras Kovacs knows perfectly well that the general public dislikes this kind of 'demystifying' film. We go back to Pierre Perrault's comments on the subject, to his total rejection of the established cinema. Perrault insists again and again:

'The mass of people isn't interested in the "living cinema", and doesn't want it. It doesn't want to live in a way that's possible, only in a way that's exciting. It doesn't like its own life. Only people who are really alive love life, people who stand up to things and don't go to the cinema. . . . We [as a whole] are beings formed by legend and fairy-tales. We want a cinema that will give answers to everything. A cinema of replacement. Not a living cinema . . . but another life, a dream-life, a pleasant little drug.' (Perrault interviewed in *Image et Son*.) Kovacs is the first man working in direct cinema who has tried to make a comparison between cinema and television and to analyse their varying effects on the audience. He thought that *The Unruly Ones*, in spite of its excessive amount of dialogue and
104

its refusal to use current cinematic practice, belonged to the cinema rather than to television: 'Television not only makes possible a composition that is very much less compact, but actually demands it. A man watching television is less capable of concentrating his attention than a man sitting in a dark cinema who has paid to see this or that particular film. I have noticed that when it is shown on television [the film] seems to have a rhythm that is too fast, even for me; details are lost and words escape one's notice.' When he considers direction Kovacs gives what seems the ideal definition of a Marxist making direct cinema films:

'Spontaneity does not exclude the possibility of a pre-arranged concept, just as scientists use hypotheses, even though sometimes one of his discoveries is due to the chance that he makes a false move. Discovery doesn't just apply to details: the details can also contribute to a relationship with things. Hasn't the artist a right to see them, to emphasise them? For us, who admit quite openly that we're committed artists, objectivity and commitment aren't irreconcilable contradictions. In fact, it's actually our socialist commitment that demands that we look reality in the face, sincerely and without pity.'

Is it a coincidence that Kovacs, like Leacock, mentions the work of scientists? The similarity of the two references is significant: for Kovacs, it is a case of scientific hypotheses; for Leacock, it is an analysis with the microscope: in the beginning was the word . . . not in the mind, but in the camera! Kovacs never did anything like this again but his later films, *Frozen Days* (1966) and *The Walls* (1968), although they reintroduced fiction and professional actors, show an increasingly sensitive use of language, of the balance of words with one another and with what they infer.

Still in Hungary, Marianna Szemes' *Divorce in Budapest* (*Valas Budapesten,* 1963) shows us couples young and old, from town or country, appearing before a court one after another to put forward their case and explain their reasons for divorcing or being reconciled. The heavy, soundless 35mm camera concentrates on the faces talking in synchronised sound. The only people filmed were those who had agreed to be. 'I can't say we learned things about divorce that we didn't know before,' said Kovacs. 'But the large number of subtle, splendid observations give the film a very great deal of interest.' In *I Plead For You* (*Erted haragszom*, 1968) Marianna Szemes tries to explain to us, through a mixture of fiction and reality, why a young student has tried to kill himself. Actors, semi-professionals or amateurs, among them the director's daughter, play roles which are close to their feelings or experience. In *Where Does Life End?* (*Meddig el az ember?*, 1968) a young woman director, Judit Elek, balances two working lives, that of an old man who is leaving his work, and that of a young man who is starting work as an apprentice. In Hungary direct cinema, which means above all a cinema of truth, tries in all honesty to lance the abscess of socialist society. One may criticise its techniques, but not its design, or its exemplary moral rigour.

Yugoslavia uses direct cinema extensively to denounce the faults of socialist society. One man dominates the scene, Kristo Skanata. He is almost unknown outside Yugoslavia and yet he deserves a reputation as high as that of Rouch or Leacock for the absolute frankness with which he treats his subjects. Filmed in direct cinema at the very heart of what is happening, his excellent films, though made with rudimentary techniques, take us into the action as it is taking place, even more than the Hungarian films do. *The First Case* shows how a miner loses an arm at work and finds himself with a ridiculously small pension. His friends quickly rally round to help and, by denouncing the privileges of a number of officials, blow up a scandal. Workers on strike in a socialist country tell us the reasons for their strike. In *Rest For the Warrior* the case of an old communist whose ideals have ended up as sclerosis and a lack of confidence in those around him, is shown through the talk of poor peasants with whom he fought in the Resistance, and through his subordinates in the factory who criticise his apathy. The film is open-ended. Skanata is a man of burning dramas, a great film-maker of action, of direct cinema in the most moral sense of the word.

Two other 'stars' exist in the socialist countries. First there is a young East German, Werner Heynowski who specialises in the denouncing interview and works in collaboration with the interviewer Gerhard Scheumann. *O.K.* makes a young countrywoman talk; she went over to the West, became barmaid in a nightclub for Americans, realised her mistake and returned to the 'good' Germany. In *The Man Who Laughs* (*Der lachende Mann*) an old German mercenary from the Congo, sozzled with whisky, talks about his crimes quite candidly in a Munich studio; in *Piloten im Pyjama* eight American pilots detained in Vietnam are interviewed for four hours. Heynowski, fired by malicious anger, alters whatever he uses and plays tricks with direct cinema with all the talent of a polemicist who denounces even the truth of direct cinema. Then there is the Pole, Kasimir Karabasz, who has admitted to being very much influenced by 'free cinema' and who represents a whole very lively Polish school of direct cinema which deserves more detailed consideration.

The other great socialist country using direct cinema is obviously Czechoslovakia which, apart from old documentary efforts like Rudolph Cincera's *Romeo and Juliet* (a performance of the play), Pavel Brezina's *Potlatch* (youngsters from Prague, all dressed up, set off to spend a weekend living like real American cowboys), has produced a new school in fiction that was born from direct cinema and uses actors who are often not professionals. According to Milos Forman who made *Peter and Pavla*, *A Blonde in Love* and *The Firemen's Ball*, they were inspired by neo-realism and the 'New Wave' and wanted to show the real problems of everyday life which the official Czech cinema was no longer accustomed to show. In 1962 Forman made *Competition* in 16mm, starting from shots for a 'candid cinema', and with a slender plot: young Czechs dream of becoming pop-singers and thus improving their position in life. Forman slightly forces the tone and situations in order to show the caricaturish side of what he was saying, and this tendency increased in his full-length films. In *Something Else*, Vera Chytilova, with mathematical rigour and the help of words and sound, gave a double portrait of a female sports champion and of a nonchalant housewife; and the sportswoman was a real Olympic champion, Eva Bosakova. In *Courage for Every Day* Ewald Schorm had two excellent professional actors, Jana Brejchova and Jan Kacer, but also used all the resources of direct cinema (or 'through contact', as people say in Prague) to increase the sounds in the place he was filming and to make the intolerable tension of the situation seem more real. In his *Intimate Lighting*, Ivan Passer, who generally worked with Forman, almost slipped into naturalism in his effort to define the greyness of country life in a forgotten village. The young Czech cinema, following the early Truffaut and De Sica, modestly tries to stick to reality. Here, direct cinema means a basic simplicity and familiarity, and a return to the everyday; which, for Czechoslovakia, is in its way revolutionary.

The Political Essay

In some special cases, when a great event takes place, the force of direct cinema lies, quite simply, in the fact that it can testify to, and can catch the intensity of, a moment in history, often with quite anonymous collaboration from others. Two films come to mind, one tainted with propaganda, yet with enough fragmentary occurrences for it to qualify as a piece of historical testimony, the other short, snapshot-style, and quite without frills. The first is *August 18 in An Tien-Men Square*, a film in colour with synchronised sound brought out by the studios of the People's Republic of China; the second has no title, and so I am calling it *Return to the Wonder Factories After the Strike*. The Chinese film, as its title suggests, celebrates the youthful enthusiasm of the cultural revolution at its start when, on August 18 1966, hundreds of thousands of young people, with red scarves round their necks, red standards flying, and carrying their little red books, cheered President Mao Tse-tung, surrounded by his cabinet, chief of which were Marshal Lin Piao and Prime Minister Chou En-lai. The film came out almost the day after this event and reached Europe in October. Here we saw Mao Tse-tung go up to the official rostrum led by a little girl and looking like a symbol of history itself. Farther off, Chou En-lai was mixing with a group of young people and got them to start singing a hymn to the glory of the revolution, while he himself puffed and sweated. These few functional images (which it would be all too easy to compare with *Parteitag* in Hitler's time), in which an entire communist crowd communicated with its leader, show
108

us, without words, but with sound and colour, the shock
that struck China in 1966; they incarnate the fervour of
the Chinese people, united to a man, from the leaders to the
youngest Pioneer. *Return to the Wonder Factories After the
Strike* shows what happened early in June 1968 when, after the
anarchical uprising of French students and young workers in
May, work was resumed; and those who believed everything
was going to be different were filled with bitterness. We see a
dark young woman employed at the Wonder factory refusing
to go back to work as two young trade unionists are urging her
to do by repeating their leaders' slogans: 'The working class
can return to its factories with its head held high.' A white-
haired man of sixty comes out of a small factory door onto
the pavement, and asks those who are going to return to work
to get back to the shop-floor. The young woman bursts into
tears and expresses her indignation. In only ten minutes the
tension of a historical period has been summed up more force-
fully than it could be in any other medium; in such a case,
cinema and television can only act as one.

Return to the Wonder Factory After the Strike is the first
French film which, in its elemental sense, contains the essential part of Leacock's message without the smallest sign of
plagiarism. For the cinema can, and must, turn over a new
page.

In these two cases, one cannot speak of a 'political essay' in
the sense that we shall seek to define it later; yet the fact that
the cinema has dealt with such subjects means that one cannot
rationalise it away from politics. *The Unruly Ones* could in a
sense be called a direct cinema political essay; but I would not
say that Mikhail Romm's *Ordinary Fascism* (1965), mentioned
earlier, came into the category of political films. In it, with the
help of documents of the time, Romm tries to link yesterday's
obvious fascism with today's latest brand of fascism, which is
invisible to the naked eye. The strongest moments are supposed
to be those in which, with the sound cut out, Hitler grimaces
before an ecstatic crowd. One must say insistently that if the
Germans in the thirties had known Hitler only by that grotesque face they would never have supported him to a man as
they did. Those of us who still remember the newsreels and
radio broadcasts of the time, bringing us the uproar at the huge

109

National-socialist meetings, can all too well remember the shrieking madman who chilled us to the marrow.

The political films we are going to mention are films conceived entirely in sound and language with an amazing boldness, love of danger and feeling of defiance. We shall try to see their human meaning beyond politics, and to see just where the artist's romanticism, even when he is profoundly committed, stumbles over history.

Early in June 1968 Fernando Solanas, a young Argentinian who had worked in television, and had already made several hundred short advertising films, turned out a massive film, four and three quarter hours long. The title, *La Hora de los Hornos* (literally 'The Hour of the Ovens'), referred to the hero of Latin-American independence, José Marti, and it was used by the Cuban leader Che Guevara in his message to the so-called Tri-continental assembly, in 1967. The ovens referred to are the lights seen in the old days by sailors as they came in to land, glimmers from ovens signalling the presence of Indians. By analogy the oven became the brazier, the signal for the great uprising. For three years, in their spare time, Solanas and his collaborator Octavio Getino collected an amazing number of documents, actual events of the time, and interviews. The film is divided into three parts. The first part, sub-divided into thirteen notes and a prologue, is inspired a great deal by the techniques of advertising films and Soviet 'agit-prop'. Everything explains how the colonialism of earlier centuries has been followed by a neo-colonialism in which culture, as well as the economy, plays a very important part. Solanas castigates the passivity of the bourgeoisie, synthesising the protest of thousands of Latin American intellectuals against the present order of things. This first part acquires all its weight from what comes after it; on its own, it fails to convince. The audience is manipulated and provoked rather than led on to reflect. The second part, 'Action for liberation' (120 minutes) really gives the film its meaning. The tone changes radically. No more editing for effect and no more large titles. Instead we have language – the words of students of all kinds, the words of trade unionists at work or in the underground movement. Then we enter the political essay, properly speaking, when Solanas seeks to show *peronismo* as the working class's awareness for the first time of

110

its own unity and strength. This part, at least the version of it shown at Pesaro, opens with some remarkable images of the planes shooting at the crowds gathered round Perón. Solanas develops his theory, a theory sustained by striking images: one class takes over from another and the bourgeoisie seizes power. All the rest of the second part shows the fall of Perón and its consequences. Ideas which today find their echo, both in Europe and elsewhere, among fascist sympathisers make this defence and illustration of *peronismo* seem profoundly shocking. Not that Solanas cares: by the use of words which he gathers everywhere – not just from one side – he makes us see more and more the hope that *peronismo* represented and still represents in the memories of the people, a hope now justified by the present state of the country. A trade unionist supporter of Perón, pursued by the police, talks from the place where he was left for dead. Behind the grills of an occupied factory the strikers sing of their hopes. Solanas seems about to start preaching. But language, language alone, the true word, takes one's breath away, forces one to reflect and elaborate one's own ideas. The third part, which is the shortest, is an appeal to action, and will be completed by all the testimonies that are still to come.

La Hora de los Hornos raises problems that are too serious not to demand a detailed analysis, but this is impossible within the framework of this book. I will try simply to show its grandeur as a work of the cinema, and its dangers in relation to living reality. Solanas does not try to cheat, and sets his film on the level of history in the making. His subtle argument presupposes a very detailed analysis and understanding of the present state of affairs in South America and, more widely, throughout the whole of America. In the emotive style of direct cinema, he invites us to look and, even more, to understand. The weakness of the first part lies in the fact that it could be used for pretty well any cause: with a few modifications and with cutting that simplifies what is being said, it could prove anything or nothing. But as soon as the discussions begin, all that they imply becomes clear; when fragments of real events from the past are used, and contemporary events as well, events that are full of revolutionary meaning simply because they are the reflection of history in the making, then it is

111

impossible to shut one's eyes and ears. The reassuring Soviet cinema of the twenties, taking place *after* the event, is over and done with: here, history is being made at the same time as the film, and sometimes the film actually outstrips history. How far can the film-maker's commitment go? This is the serious question asked by a masterly film of this kind. One can imagine the Marxes and Lenins, the Roosevelts and de Gaulles of the future, writing their reflections on history past and future with this lightweight, omnipresent synchronised camera that plunges us into reality in the making. Solanas, who studied music, composes a remarkable sound accompaniment, mixing sounds and music in a rather 'concrete' way – using the word in the sense that Pierre Schaeffer gives it when referring to concrete music; he also quite often holds the camera himself and so links events with words very closely. *La Hora de los Hornos* is a wild, excited and exciting film which should be seen and judged calmly and coolly. Only thus can we know where we are going after such a film, which is ambitious enough and revolutionary enough in its use of sound to recall the age of Eisenstein and Dziga Vertov. I do not say it is better than their films, or less good; it is certainly quite different. After it our ideas of the cinema as an art or as a medium, and of its role in society, must be radically reconsidered.

The work of Emile de Antonio is as burningly contemporary, and in the same way urges us to reconsider radically the basis of the traditional cinema; each film must be considered in the context of its own time. Three films in which montage, in the widest sense of the word, played an important part, began his career: *Point of Order* (co-director Dan Talbot, 1962), *Rush to Judgement* (1967) and *In the Year of the Pig* (1968). In a long interview published in the autumn/winter 1967 number of *Film Comment* (New York) de Antonio talks in detail about his late arrival on the film scene and about the kind of cinema that interests him. 'My experience of the cinema goes back over the last five years,' he says. 'I came to this new medium as an intellectual, a university teacher and literary adviser to a publishing house; fundamentally I am a man of words who has taught philosophy and literature but I also have an interest in modern art, particularly in the *avant-garde* and in visual imagery.' *Point of Order*, his first film, was a montage cut down

112

from twenty-eight hours of kinescope bought from the CBS company, showing people representing the American army under attack from Senator Joseph McCarthy from April 22 to June 16 1964. '*Point of Order*,' de Antonio says in his interview, 'is centred on what interests me most philosophically, the defeat of American culture . . . McCarthyism is the triumph of publicity – which says absolutely nothing, but does so with the consummate talent McCarthy possessed.' The film, even if it is presented as a fairly logical narrative, has no chronology ('Everything was taken out of context, to make what at the time I considered an actual trial'.) Some judged it one way, some another, and it condemns not only the infamous witch-hunter McCarthy, but Joseph Welch, the lawyer on the opposite side who, with his coolness and the liveliness of his answers, made Joe McCarthy lose his head and fall in the estimation of twenty million American television viewers who were following the trial live. According to de Antonio it was not a case of angel and devil, but merely of two demagogues confronting each other. 'Joseph Welch was a right-wing republican, and in the film he finally approaches people in the same way as McCarthy. Welch was no hero, he was simply a brilliant tactician, a great man of the law and a fantastic actor – a man whose dramatic talent was unquestionable even if his morality was dubious.' De Antonio admits how depressed he was by the first reactions of the critics, even though they were very favourable. '*Point of Order* was mainly attacking the idea of complicity, the American Establishment, the army's weakness – Stevens and Adams and all those stupid generals. Of course, it was also an attack on McCarthy, but not on McCarthy any more than on the others.' The most remarkable thing about this film, made entirely from images by television cameras taken in a senate committee-room, is that without breaking the rules of the game it imprisons the audience in the unity of place and, I would add, within the unity of a single point of view; yet it is certainly direct cinema *par excellence*, because the entire action is based upon language, language used, emphasised, contrasted, to produce an absurd meaning out of the whole comedy, Senator McCarthy not necessarily being the biggest buffoon. The end of the film, in which MacCarthy loses his nerve as a melodramatic climax, is pure invention by de Antonio.

Rush to Judgement is signed by Emile de Antonio alone but takes the title of the book published by the lawyer Mark Lane just before the film was shown, and has Mark Lane taking part in the narrative as defence counsel. The film needs someone to plead for Lee Harvey Oswald, killed by Jack Rubin in a Dallas gaol and thought by the Warren Commission to be guilty of the assassination of President Kennedy on November 27 1963, without having really been tried. 'The defence lawyer has no alternative theory to offer; he can only point out that the facts used against his client are not consistent.' In the above-mentioned interview de Antonio said: 'It is a kind of Brechtian cinema; it is the theatre of facts, the theatre of argument, the theatre of judicial investigation, the theatre of attack against the establishment and the government. It is a burning topic.' On another occasion he said: 'The film, the magnetic tape, the camera, the tape recorder and the moviola on which I show the film are neutral – when I'm not using them. They are as neutral as a gun. Or as a typewriter.' And in the same interview he goes on: '. . . in this film, the central problem is that of total credibility. I don't say we invent credibility, but we do sacrifice everything to it, we even sacrifice dramatic interest in order to present our arguments.' This, perhaps, is what really struck the audiences. The film is divided into two parts. The first part shows the assassination itself, the second, more broadly, the corrupt atmosphere of Dallas. Witnesses mentioned in the film were not heard by the Warren Commission, or rather their testimony was cut. De Antonio, in an austere, anti-cinemato-graphic, unrhythmical style, with photography that is sometimes merely undistinguished, gives us a remarkable account of the values and the system that underpin contemporary America, at least as it is seen from Texas. The film disturbed the American desire for conformity: it appealed so little to the attractive and the reassuring, in both its contents and its images, that it was a failure. But it remains historical testimony.

In the Year of the Pig might be called *Mr Smith Goes to Vietnam* in memory of Frank Capra and, like Capra's famous film, it is bathed entirely in a purely American idealism, yet broadened by all the forcefulness of direct cinema and strengthened by an even more burning subject than those of de Antonio's earlier films – on the war in Vietnam.

De Antonio was not making cheap propaganda film but showing the absurdity of this war through an authentically eloquent form of cinema, with a dense, meaningful language. There was no propagandist talk, but past declarations borrowed from television, or present-day ones obtained specially for the film, kept being compared. In a way, *In the Year of the Pig* takes the line of *Point of Order*; it is a vigorous film pamphlet, which pitilessly analyses the absurd politics involved: absurd politics that have cost hundreds of thousands of lives. The dialogue sometimes fuses with the rhythm of a machine-gun; two sentences put together and contrasted may form a unit as explosive as the best 'montage of attractions' used by Eisenstein and the silent cinema. But this time people speak. With a terrifying sobriety, the film ends with images of dead and wounded men such as we have never seen before. Probably de Antonio would still have the right to talk about Brechtian cinema if these images of the dead were not so ambiguous; all of them are killed no matter what the cause, and all have reached *the end*. But Brecht – the Brecht of *Baal*, and of *Mother Courage* – would in the end have agreed with de Antonio.

The Unknown Third World

Before speaking of the Third World cinema we must define what we mean by the Third World. The result is bound to be very modest: we shall bring together information collected in Rio de Janeiro, Tunis and Beirut, discussions held with Brazilian film-makers, Africans from black Africa or Arabs, and the opinions of Europeans who know Africa – whether they are film-makers or not: men like Jacques Berque, Jean Rouch and Gerald Belkin, Canadian by birth and French by adoption. The Third World is all the civilisations, all the states – old or new – that have only partially enjoyed the Western-style consumer society as it has emerged in the capitalist countries of Europe and North America, and to a certain extent in the socialist countries of Europe; or else have not enjoyed it at all. Now that the gap grows wider between those who have everything, indeed too much, and those who are seeking to have just a little, or who sometimes even dream of creating a different kind of society – one that is closer to their own traditions – people have a right to consider what benefit the cinema could bring to the Third World and, more particularly, the direct cinema we are dealing with.

Edgar Morin, who almost unconditionally admires direct films like Karel Reisz's *We Are the Lambeth Boys* of British 'free cinema', and Andras Kovacs' *The Unruly Ones* (see the earlier section entitled 'Socialism in Direct Cinema'), in September 1965 in Rio de Janeiro defined both the importance of direct cinema to a sociologist who wished to take sociology out of the universities, and the role which it already played in a country like Brazil, which will serve us as a model, or rather as a point of reference, for the whole of the Third World. He said:

'Direct cinema means diving into the reality of things. And, for that reason, it is a reality which I consider irreplaceable. In direct cinema the director goes straight for the actual problems of life. In confronting them he must take up an attitude that dialectically unites impersonal observation and personal participation. The truth presented by *cinéma-vérité*[1] is the result of this dialectic between objectivity of observation and the director's subjective intervention. From this we may conclude that direct cinema's method is a synthesis of two methods: the gathering of testimonies from people questioned and the scientifically directed intervention of the director. There can be no pure, cold objectivity in this. In direct cinema there is always an element of provocation. Leacock's cinema, for instance, seeks to "testify". Yet the cinema is a tool that penetrates reality and can, of course, go further . . . Direct cinema is, above all, an instrument of communication. It seeks closer communication with life and a fuller communication with the public. Once again, direct cinema has contributed to the education of Brazilian directors of full-length films. The whole Brazilian cinema is trying to become a cinema of communication. This need for communication has found an ethical, aesthetic and economic solution in direct cinema.' (Text which appeared in *Cinelandia*, September 27 1965.)

[1] See analysis of Edgar Morin's *cinéma vérité* in the section entitled 'The Forerunners'.

This declaration is bursting with meaning and inference as well as a certain lack of understanding, on which we will not dwell, of Leacock's work; this lack of understanding is neither more nor less revealing than the ignorance which Christian Metz and Marshal MacLuhan have shown about the fundamental problems of expression in the modern cinema. But two essential points must be made: direct cinema, even in Edgar Morin's version of it – slightly poorer, that is, than American or Canadian direct cinema – is the ideal instrument of communication in a country like Brazil; and the Brazilian *cinema novo* in fiction,[1] is direct cinema's putative child. A great deal has already been written about what has been done in direct cinema in Brazil. An important joint experiment was made in the Department of Mass Communications in the University of Brasilia. Nelson Pereira dos Santos, director of the very fine film *Vidas Secas* (1964), inspired by Graciliano Ramos' novel about the poverty of the north-eastern region of Brazil, was involved in the section on cinema, together with Paolo Emilio Salles Gomez, a critic and essayist well known in Sao Paolo. In an interview published in *Cinema 67*, No. 112, he explains the work he did with his pupils in the following way:

'We made a film, *Fala, Brasilia* (*Speak, Brasilia*). It is a film of linguistic research, because the town of Brasilia is a real laboratory from the point of view of language in Brazil. Its population is made up of people of every region in Brazil. In the Portuguese spoken in Brazil there are differences of vocabulary and differences of sound. The pronunciation and even the vocabulary vary. These films of ours were made with the students, after a great deal of research, under the direction of a specialist in dialects. They are not scientific films, they are meant to be popular films.'

This clearly suggests direct cinema, even though equipment that would allow satisfactory work to be done was unobtainable.[2] Synchronised sound that worked with 16mm or 35mm

[1] See chapter entitled 'The Birth of Young Cinemas'.
[2] On this subject see *Le Tournage en direct au Brésil* by Julio A. Mendes, published by Unesco in 1965; and *La Découverte de la spontanéité* by David Neves (Rio, Centre Latin-Américain, 1965).

117

always gives rise to serious problems because of the lack of development of laboratories and studios. Glauber Rocha, the most famous Brazilian director of fiction films, directs in what I think is the spirit of direct cinema even though synchronised sound is impossible to achieve. The language used in *Black God, White Devil* is stylised, at once literary and ethnographically exact; just as the research into customs and history demanded both strict realism and poetic transposition. At the end of 1965, before undertaking *Terra am Transe*, Rocha tried to make a film in 16mm with synchronised sound in the Amazon region, but insurmountable technical difficulties seem to have stopped him. Nelson Pereira dos Santos, in the interview already mentioned, goes a little further on the use of synchronised sound and expresses anxieties much like those of Pierre Perrault and Jean Rouch.

'It is very important for the documentary and also for the fiction film, the full-length film. We have always had a problem over the dialogue of films, and I am speaking of full-length ones. In our country there is a very clear difference between the spoken and the written language, that is, between the Portuguese language, which is used only for writing, and the language of the people. In showing ordinary people, one sometimes puts into their mouths a language they have never spoken . . . People in the street nearly always make mistakes, and they are not faults of pronunciation; people talk too fast, you can't understand them, even in real life. What counts isn't how people speak, because before they speak they've got to think; what counts is the way people think and how their thought reaches lingusitic expression. That is what matters most and it is that which we have learnt from direct cinema.'

A second interview, that of the documentary-maker Sergio Muniz, published in *Image et Son*, June/July 1968, sums up a directly human aspect of creation in Brazil which applies in many countries in the Third World, particularly in black Africa. Sergio Muniz is talking about a short film he means to make which he believes in deeply – *Rastejador*:

'It is the story of a man in the days of the *cangaceiros*, who could see if anyone had passed that way by clues invisible to the layman; and he could tell if one person or two had passed and whether on horseback or on foot. I went to see this man, Rastejador, in a number of places in the *sertao*. One day he said to me: "You know where you're walking? See these trees, these cactus plants?" Then he showed me a small green leaf: "Green leaves don't fall. Someone must have passed this way and damaged the green leaves. It may have been a cow, or a deer, or an armed man on foot." In the same way he'd tell you that a man who was blind in his left eye came this way. It is an almost empirical perception of nature. He knew the traditions in which to survive in the *sertao*, where to find water, what you could eat: "This plant is good, that one's bad, that's poison." It will be an ethnographical film on the means of survival in the *sertao*. I want to make this film because I think it's important for those who come after us.'

Sergio Muniz then established a clear distinction between the research film made for a specialised audience and the popular film made for a large audience. But before starting to film one must have at least the rudiments of equipment. In 1965, in Rio, Claude Jutra of Canada and I suggested that cooperation should be established between Canada, which was overdeveloped in matters of direct cinema, and Brazil. At about the same time, David Neves, at the conclusion of his report, proposed 'the creation, through Unesco (by agreement with cultural organisations in the various countries), of regional centres to produce films of technical, social and anthropological research. America could be considered one of these regions, with Brazil, for instance, forming a centre.'

Direct cinema documentaries show what can be done with the means available. Consider, first of all, Leon Hirszman's *Maioria Absoluta* (1964), on the poverty of the peasants in north-east Brazil, and Geraldo Sarno's *Viramundo* (1965), on the migration of peasants from the north-east to Sao Paolo where they hope that the wheel of fortune may eventually turn in their favour. Although Brazil is an underdeveloped country in which millions of people are hungry, it is quite highly

119

developed in its cinema compared with many other countries
of the Third World where no cinema at all exists. Gerald Belkin,
back from Tanzania where he had been preparing a film, gave
a warning about this: people, he suggested, talk so subtly about
poverty that they forget the fact of poverty itself. He felt that
national African cinemas could not be simple consumer
cinemas as they are in Europe or America. The African countries are poor, they have little money available, and it is absurd
to seek solutions that are quite beyond their means, such as the
setting up of a film centre at a cost of 800,000 dollars, as the
Tanzanians were advised to do by a Canadian expert who,
even after two years of study, did not understand the real
priorities. Today Tanzania is turning to the east which, however, does not provide the most suitable material. Like Jean
Rouch, Gerald Belkin thinks that the cheap 16mm with
synchronised sound is the best solution for an African cinema.
With it, people would hear the language of their own countries
spoken, they would be able to get the physical feel of their
country, its weight, its size, its real appearance. All cinema
should be considered in relation to the general development of
the country; a film should not prevent a school being built.
The cinema is necessary, but those who have to take decisions
often know nothing about the technical and economic factors
involved in making it. Those responsible naturally have a tendency to put forward old ideas which are not necessarily the best.

Jacques Berque, speaking of the cinema in the Arab world,
raises a more theoretical problem;[1] the choice between literary
Arabic, which is understood only by literate people but in all
Arab countries, and popular Arabic, which varies from country
to country; between the classical language and dialect. Jean
Rouch, in his study *Present-Day Situation and Tendencies in
the African Cinema* (1962; he is dealing with black Africa), also
brings up the problems of language, and of the innumerable
dialects that mean a film must have a number of sound tracks
in order to be understood in a single country. This brings us
back to the myth of the tower of Babel, as direct cinema in
general does, and to Marshal McLuhan and his idea of

[1] In *Les Cinémas des pays Arabes* edited by Georges Sadoul and published in Beirut in 1966.

retribalisation. It is impossible not to be angry, as Belkin is, at the civilised world's indifference to the Third World, at its inability to lay the foundations for useful collaboration between the advanced and the underdeveloped countries. What we should export is not our way of thinking but the tools and the method of using them so that each country can make the best use of them and find its own original voice. Jean Rouch in Niger with the outlook of a European long familiar with Africa, Ousmane Sembène in Senegal, his own country, with experience acquired in the Soviet Union and in France, Mustapha Alasanne in Niger, who has worked at the National Film Board in Montreal – each gives an answer of a kind. In any country life itself must come before art.

After Brecht and the Living Theatre

This analysis of direct cinema has a meaning only if it goes further than mere reporting to what can really be called narrative – that is, a realist art full of new meanings, using what Luc de Heusch, in his study *Cinéma et sciences sociales* (published by Unesco, 1962), calls (*à propos* Robert Flaherty) the 'participating camera'. Jean Rouch uses this definition in the chapter he wrote on the ethnographic film for the volume *Ethnologie Générale*, recently published by the Encyclopédie de la Pléiade. At its highest level of achievement Richard Leacock's direct cinema is, first of all, a revived technique recording reality, in which the cameraman becomes a new type of worker altogether – not self-absorbed and self-sufficient and not wanting his images to be too polished; a man who shoots for sound and, after shooting, cuts his own film. Pierre Perrault also creates an autonomous form of dramatic art that starts with the direct registration of reality and an autonomous method of shooting; thus, direct cinema becomes the creator of new sorts of fiction, or rather of new dimensions in fiction, not exactly 'cinema' in the usual sense, but not the theatre, the novel, or the radio either.

If we have come to consider what is familiar and everyday with a new kind of eyesight and to reject the alienating, idealising fiction that has so far held sway in the cinema (popular, as in the case of Michel Audiard, or intellectual, as in the case of

121

Antonioni), and as a result to reject as well the stories and language they use (too obvious in the case of Audiard, too symbolic in the case of Antonioni); then we find the fundamental demands that Brecht and the Berliner Ensemble, and later Julian Beck and the Living Theatre, made in radically different contexts and with radically different methods, bursting through the limitations of the old theatre and declaring that a more 'participating' art was needed, closely linked with the society in which we live. Bertolt Brech with his Marxist background thought that the aim of the theatre was to criticise society, to show that nothing – and certainly not injustice and poverty – just grew out of itself; that man, man first of all, could create a better world, in order to do which he must keep fighting against nature and must overcome and enslave it first of all within himself. Décor, costume, diction and music all help to increase the audience's awareness, to make it see through its intelligence and its heart that it is not seeing merely an isolated story, an anecdote, but a very small part of a much larger whole that is the history of man.

The actor was obviously of primary importance to Brecht the author and director. Brecht was familiar with the cinema; during his exile in America he saw as many films as he could and, being a great reader of detective stories, took an interest in thrillers in the cinema. As far as the theory of the cinema was concerned he believed in its possibilities of illustration but hesitated to put forward any risky ideas. I would call his ideas on the cinema post-expressionist. He gave the actor in the theatre very precise instructions: 'The man from Augsbourg [Brecht was a native of Augsbourg] filmed Weigel [his wife, the actress Helen Weigel] while she put on her make-up. He cut the film and each image showed a finished facial expression, sufficient to itself and with its own meaning . . . Those to whom he showed these pictures, asking what the various expressions meant, suggested things like anger, gaiety, envy, pity. He showed them to Weigel as well, telling her only that she should know her own expressions in order to be able to express a number of moods without necessarily having to feel them.' (*Dialogues on the Copper Sale*, 'Third night, effect A'.) Here is a possible way in which the silent cinema might be used in the training of actors for the theatre, a device that would allow an actor to

122

acquire greater mastery of his own expression quite independently of the work done on the text and of the text's meaning. Moreover, the Brechtian actor does not perform realistically in the bourgeois sense of the word (we know the importance Brecht gave to the techniques of the oriental theatre).

Where, then, can we put this discreet transition from acting pure and simple, from the rendering of the text, to the meaningful language with all its impact, its contents, its melody and its rhythm? For Brecht this meaning could come only from the actor's hard work on the character he was playing, the subject of the play, and its relationship with history.

But in direct cinema, and first of all in Leacock's films, reality is given to us raw with all its instant, provocative qualities. Unlike Brecht's theatre, which rejects the fake realism of the bourgeois theatre and seeks to give us social reality by distancing the audience from the stage and the action, Leacock's cinema, denouncing the fake realism of what is said to be the only possible cinema – that of performance – moving us to take a more intense part in real action, gives us the tool needed to discover on the screen how things *really* happen. Here 'reality' can be seen at first glance, if it has been filmed with the right skill. Then the social fiction that underpins all our actions can be revealed, the drama we act out each day for society. By this new relationship with the lightweight synchronised camera, the person filmed, whether an actor or not, appears to our eyes and ears in a new dimension. Finally we begin to respond to the amazing challenge flung at us by Julian Beck and the Living Theatre in *Paradise Now*, in which you and I and all of us are invited to enter the game and strip the old man who is a prisoner of social constraints. In the cinema nothing is ever written in advance and so everything is possible. Like rediscovering how man builds up his life from day to day, how public and private life cannot be divided, how every day we submit while time, objects and passions are consumed. In other words, it is possible to forget the written word in favour of the living, lived word, flung out by man *en situation*.

CONCRETE CINEMA

Concrete Cinema

Pierre Schaeffer, in his short book, *La Musique concrète* (1967), gives us a first definition of this form of music with which his name, even more than Pierre Henry's,[1] is linked:

'We can compare exactly the two directions taken by music: the abstract and the concrete. We have already said that the adjective "abstract" can be applied to conventional music because it is first of all conceived in the spirit, then noted theoretically, and finally realised by being played on an instrument. We have called our music 'concrete' because it is made up of elements that already exist, borrowed from any kind of sound material, either a noise or a musical note, then composed musically by direct construction, tending to achieve a definite composition without the aid, which has grown impossible, of ordinary musical notation.'

Let us replace 'conventional music' by 'conventional cinema', 'sound material' by 'visual and sound material', 'noise or musical note' by 'realistic or elaborated image', and we have the basis for a possible 'concrete cinema', defined like this not in a facile and imitative way but in order to emphasise the originality of this contemporary and fairly recent form of cinema, in comparison with the realistic, classical cinema. In opposition to this naturalistic rather than realistic cinema, which catches a diminished form of reality, there is direct cinema on the one hand and its intensified participation in what is happening, as in Richard Leacock's films, a participation renewed and enriched by all sorts of verbal subtleties and by sound that is truly synchronous; and on the other hand a cinema that is

[1] They composed together, most notably *Symphonie pour un homme seul* (1950) on which Maurice Béjart based a famous ballet which he danced to his own choreography.

127

entirely synthetic, entirely formed through man's craft. The temptation, then, is to call this latter cinema 'concrete'

In concrete cinema nothing is left to chance, everything is entirely deliberate and elaborated, often in a craftsmanlike way. Pierre Schaeffer himself, in his research team of the ORTF, gave *carte blanche* to the two disciplines, direct and concrete, on equal terms. Many directors of so-called animated films have been tempted by direct cinema; the first of them was Walerian Borowczyk, since he made *Rosalie*, in which the modulated words of his wife Lijia, who plays the main part, are sometimes used with animation effects, and objects are manipulated. In both techniques the real weight of things must be felt.

Concrete cinema, then, includes animation and, more generally, the American underground, which is not widely known. The Americans sought to make creation in the cinema so individual that it would be as immediate and tangible as the work of the painter with his brush, the sculptor with his chisel, or the composer with his notes. It is hardly surprising that concrete cinema is often the work of painters, sculptors and musicians.

Technique and Work[1]

The brief notes that follow are inspired by an implicit method which we will not go into deeply here. Equally, the text and the films dealt with are not, as Joyce said of *Finnegan's Wake*, 'fragments but active elements', which 'when they are more numerous, will start to fuse'. Our first hypothesis is that, like every art, the cinema will reveal itself if we reduce its basic conditions, if these conditions are 'made effective'. Here, as an example, we are going to start from the screen;[2] the world put forward by the film is to be born from the struggle against the planification and the cutting symbolised by the screen. Films then tell a sort of story; they are the cinema of cinema.

Description of the screen. A screen is a plane surface. A screen is a big canvas hung up, a cloth or sheet, the result, then, of

[1] This section is by Nicole Rouzet-Albagli.

[2] The method used here takes us back to some kind of unconscious process at work in film-making. The screen is, in fact, the most external and symbolic part of film technique.

the act of weaving. Is it the final version of the tapestry? This hangs from sky to earth, and the canvas is crisscrossed with threads, across and down. But 'paradise' comes from *'parada'*, which means tapestry. And weaving is linked with the weather, if we may believe the ancient mythologies that linked weaving and spinning with fertility rites and moon worship. In Western mythology the movements by which a carpet is made correspond to the movements of the three Fates (intersection, knotting, cutting). It is thus that we must understand tapestry, in which the needle knots the thread of time and reunites time and the world.[1]

Doubly symbolic, then, is the movement that comes later – that of painting on canvas; in a way that is more or less direct, more or less faithful, the painter cuts transversally across the canvas. This symbol, taken in the pure state when the act is instantaneous (the spot of paint), reduces the canvas as a stratification of time to nothing. Except that the painter paints *on* the canvas and he paints the world. The relationship of the painting to the canvas will be more or less fundamental according to how much the canvas reveals its ambivalent function, which is to hide and to reveal.

If we ignore this function, the canvas *becomes a screen*.[2] The canvas makes itself a screen by effacing the memory of its weaving, by becoming a simple plane surface.

On this screen, as in Plato's cave, we see images unroll. Not from right to left, nor from left to right, but starting from a place behind us, at the back of the hall, from a luminous strip in which specks of dust may be whirling; and, as a rule, coming down from above. The screen means permanent images: it does not go with them and, if it stays there, it is more than the frame of a photograph. As it is what stays still while the images keep moving, it is like the very home of movement. (What does not pass in time is the passage of time itself, as Merleau-Ponty says.) Our eyes follow not the passage of each image but the movement of the succession of images. A syncopated movement which the film will take as its theme. The fact that the screen does not go away with the image

---

[1] Compare wool-spinners' songs like *'Tire, tire, l'aigille, ma fille, demain tu te maries'* and stories like *The Sleeping Beauty*.

[2] Like a memory.

means that the screen preserves the image. The images take over the screen, the world moves under our motionless eyes. Everything suggests that the only inhabited place is the living screen, that the only real thing in the hall is the film, the screen. Yet the physical presentation of a film is not enough to captivate us entirely: a still shot from a motionless camera showing us a world moving under our motionless eyes is boring. When the film stops we have to adapt ourselves, however slightly, to the cinema seats, the exit, the street. It is because here our eyes and heads are moving. We get out of the fixed frame, our eyes follow some vanishing object. It is only the projection of the images that gives the screen its fixity as an object.

Another movement enters into things and gives them life: the movement of the camera which follows the movements of reality. What captivates us is the rhythm of images, the multiple movement in which images are taken. Now the time of the film being shown becomes the time of the images. The light on the screen owes its existence to the action, which describes the world. For the projection is not a thick paste spread on the canvas. It has no thickness: it seems it barely takes shape. It comes from a distance, and it goes elsewhere. Yet it has time. It takes over the screen. It makes it vanish. And by abolishing the reality of the screen the images take on the density of real things. The film begins.

From the audience's point of view, when the screen is abolished so is the hall. Light appears on the screen when it is extinguished in the hall. In our traditional cinemas, a door half opening on to a lighted passage breaks into the film far more than the shadow of someone walking in front of the projection room, outlined against the other images. Yet, when you come to think of it, however much we may be transported by the film we do not get up and try to enter *into* the screen itself.

What captivates us, then, is the fact that the physical progress of the film and the time belonging to the images are united *in a single time*. In a 'true' film we are active: with our eyes we maintain the unified tension that transforms real time into the reality of time.

As in direct cinema, reality here is a process contemporary with the very showing of it.

The film then finds the possibilities of myth; where, in order to say what things are, one says how they have come to be. Of course, every film belongs to the cinema. Maciste fights the monsters just as Juliet fights the spirits. In the final analysis every myth may be taken back to the original myth by going to the origins of myth in general. Maurice Blanchot shows that 'the event described in the narrative is not just an event that takes place in the world of the narrative but an event and a realisation of the narrative itself'.[1]

But if the film takes as its theme the way it has become realised as a film, the method gets completely covered by its object. We have a cinema of the origins. In the same way the original myth is the myth that accomplishes the genesis and discovers, 'makes effective', the word as a force. Its theme begins to look like the world, the act through which it materialises appears as a screen, or rather a monster, a frozen product of this act of demonstration, a clue we have to analyse in order to get hold of the creative act moving into the past.

In concrete cinema, as in direct cinema, it seems that what the film is projecting in its symbols is itself: the story of its creation, its technical activity, film, screen, projection, cutting, direction, mixing, etc., and the life of the camera. In Robert Lapoujade's prison the screen becomes a stone wall. The wall takes up the size of the screen. We are the prisoner who fights the wall to give reality to his images. We share his eyesight, the film being cut by fast black flickerings that coincide with the flickering of his eyelids. But the prison is greedy with time. The images have no hold on it: whatever their theme (beloved woman, joy, separation) they are filmed in the same way, from a distance. We fling ourselves against the wall of lost time where images keep being blotted out, then start up again. The struggle takes as its theme the combat of images against the screen, a combat that fails to make the world exist.

But tending to analyse the screen means bringing in light and the world, as in *Noir et Blanc* (*Black and White*), and light and sound, as in *Foules* (*Crowds*), to create meaning. Thus *Foules* restores to the screen its function as a framework. On

[1] '... and the realisation, during the time of the narrative, of the original time whose fascinating structure this performance merely crystallises'. (Maurice Blanchot, *Le Livre à venir*.)

to it the universe is flung through juxtaposed, rolling, struggling images that do not maintain their permanence and individuality but are crowded together, dealt with destructively. Does this mean torture, or terror? A single image: a shivering, naked woman's body, shown in a trance, or at any rate at the end of her tether, keeps returning as an image of truth: it is the passion of the image that cannot happen, the image violated by real treatment. On the other hand, the faces do not cry out: their open mouths bring out a primordial sound, sound as first testimony, without time or continuity. The sound qualifies the image: this sudden apparition which looks as if a storm has swept it there is called 'A'. The faces state themselves, state the word as beginning by making it 'effective', and are cut off in using this language by being made to vanish. Images rear up against the screen in hordes, attacking the way the world goes – unconscious, unfeeling, motionless – through their number and their violence. In this fight for their life some of the images are saved for a moment, emerge, settle, waver. At the same time they point out the scandal: their death itself guarantees their truth.

The essential thing about the cinema is movement . . . Thirty still seconds are impossible: the images must be made to throb . . .

Perception is not continuous, it has to be achieved through *accumulation:* there are points of impact. The eye must aim at, must hover around, the object, which is regarded in a neutral sort of way when necessary.

This is different from painting. We must consider the cinema as a form ('Gestalt'). A drawing stops, locked in an image that has stopped. In the cinema, an image is stopped (Lapoujade).

Now, we will question the relation between sound and image at this level of cinema: in *Foules*, it seems as if, through the flow of images, a continuous cry flows as well: in it, we are made to hear the equivalent of an image. Indeed, you may wonder whether, at extremes, sound does not appear as an image. Sound comes first in relation to the image: it is more enfolding, more profound. In freeing itself it makes the distance of an image possible. The screen is not merely an obstacle, it is the total impact from which the film must be born, by dissociation of the image and the sound. Sound is the weft of the screen, the liberation of the image.

132

But the realisation of events may be moderated by its own development. In Walerian Borowczyk's *Monsieur et Madame Kabal* everything is drawn, an empty, mechanical universe, apart from the coloured butterflies that fly about to the heavy sound of crumpled wings, an *enormous sound* compared with the butterflies' size and harmlessness. The whole drawing is like an image of the noise made by pulleys and winches. Or else the only thing this drawing can let loose is the noise of machines; this means that the butterflies are out of context, come from a stock of unrealisable images, their lightness seeming to suggest that they appeared spontaneously, since here analysing means crushing and grinding. Here the sound cannot free any images. Because, in fact, there is no sound: there are only noises. It is the universe of psychosis: here the origins appear so compact that they cannot be 'reduced' (analysed) except by being chomped up by jaws and machines. The origins are themselves devouring machines.

Philippe Arthuys writes on the relations between sound and images and what he says throws light on the impossibility of noise turning into sound, of the world to be born, if we apply them to the universe of *Monsieur et Madame Kabal*:

'. . . finally, what is painful is the primacy of the image. One should be able to start from music. And the film should begin from there. In fact people believe that the image is dominant. But what makes up the film's density is sound and words. As a rule, people do not know that sound is the very stuff of cinema.

'Music: instead of giving it its poetic character or envisaging it as an abstraction, it is used to emphasise the realism of situations. Suddenly the film becomes a photograph in movement. Thus music is used to reinforce realism through the sounds that have had the same function as the noises. A noise carries a meaning, it is identifiable. Sound has been treated in the same way. The question is to know how to get away from realism in the cinema.'

It seems impossible to slachen the hold which usually realism, taken as the theme of *Monsieur et Madame Kabal*, has on the cinema. By putting aside the real and 'already existing'

133

life of the world, the film-maker can seek deliberate creation, the joy of pure invention. Instead of seeking to make images in his film, he is going to use the imaginary dimension of the world.

Thus, in *L'Oiseau*, starting from a poem about a bird, the film fades out and starts again, time makes and unmakes itself, the process of birth itself is performed.

'Real movement must not be imitated,' says Lapoujade. 'It must be transposed. Between the contemplative cinema and a transposed movement joints appear that would seem to spread a new idea of reality rather better than any mechanical movement would. Basically we question the structure of the cinema in order to produce a new dimension.' And here is Borowczyk again:

'The question is not one of technique. There is something much more important than technique. Technique is nothing, creation everything, in the end. I think this now, but my films have for a long time been technical inquiries.

'One thing must be understood – that painting is different from animation. As a rule, people use conventional drawings, before they finally choose the stereotyped model. That is a sign of poverty. What we need to do is create our own conventions. In real films, relationships must be created between movements. Actors are not created. In animation, relationships and objects must all be made. Simplified drawings are used. A rarefied, simplified scheme . . . The first enjoyable thing is to take an object and put it further away, to move it around: to move objects before the camera. In order to share this pleasure with someone else, you put it on film.'

Animation, properly so-called, can then begin. The world is envisaged as something to be put back into life, and the creative enterprise of film is going to recreate the creation of the world. 'Animation is something very big. You can animate objects that are generally thought dead, you can breathe life into them . . . With animated films you can play with the elements. You can transmit the process of the creation of movements' (Borowczyk).

134

Giving life to a dead world is the theme of the film *Renaissance* in which, through the work of the film, shapeless rubbish is given form. In a great wind feathers stick on to a stuffed owl, the pages of a book are replaced, the doll is reconstituted. And yet it is a frozen universe that is going to appear to us, to be destroyed again, as if it were all a dream.

Lapoujade's *Socrates*, on the other hand, seeks to rediscover the cosmic vibration of the world. It goes right back to the earliest techniques of knowledge, when knowledge was not merely intellectual, but a way in which being was opened up to become Being. In this film things are reborn as they are in myths and, by going back to their origins, take on new life.

Mircea Eliade has said that the idea of the creation of the world is the idea of the essence of things; and, indeed, the revelation of Being *is* the creation of the world. In a world that has rusted up, become petrified and carbonised, we are shown the act of creation, and the original matter that composes it is seen as vibrant with energy.

Film then somehow shows itself showing. In this lies its greatness. It is the inventiveness of the director's vision that appears on the screen. In *Renaissance*, as in *Socrates*, it is a case of the power of montage reshaping the universe. The film tells about itself by transforming the world, but transforming the world means borrowing elements from reality. Therefore it ignores this creation of the world, does not realise creation but shows it in a symbolic way. In this creation of reality we may read the creation of film itself, without being led to it by its very momentum

In *Jeux des Anges* it seems to be a case of cinema *qua* cinema. 'Animated objects are a lie,' says Borowczyk. 'When you make a film, you realise it is a lie. You are making something and it doesn't exist. When you stop, you tell the truth and at the same time say nothing. Then you start again. So that I shall not have time to be disappointed I make another film right away to give myself the feeling that it lasts.' As far as *Jeux des Anges* is concerned one may wonder whether the technical operation of the film itself is not its theme: the stages of the operation, ending with a gliding, syncopated movement of images on the film. 'Certainly technique is basic, in a way.

135

The question is to know how to use it.' 'People saw sounds,' says R. Abellio; at a deeper level than that of objective perception, sound and image are one.

Jeux des Anges may tell us the truth about the cinema: the impossibility of a universe of angels, of true mediation, of the unity of life, light and the world; what is left is an indifferent essence, and the screen persists as a kind of axe, the equivalent of the film frame; before the film passes on it has to stop, before birth there must be death into life.

For myth as such never creates the world. It recreates it through words and images. It behaves as if the world did not exist, but that 'as if' spoils it from the start, and this spoiling is the theme of myths. The time of genesis, when we move towards the achievement of birth where things begin to begin, towards the final stage where the history of the world can at last start, is also the time that consumes the myth, and leads us towards the end of the film. The more the film progresses the nearer comes the time when the lights will go up in the cinema: but the day that is heralded is not the one on which the lights will go up, and the screen's silence, the world's silence, are again divided.

Perhaps this is what Borowczyk's *Gavotte* shows: with music by Rameau, the film, under the guise of a gnome, cannot take place. It threshes about, becomes confused, the image is not in the same rhythm as the sound. The monster is already there, frozen living product of the act of demonstration come to life. An 'image of death'. The act of creation not realised but looked at squarely. Demonstration trying to reach itself under the guise of the world. This produces the film's ceaselessly cut irony; the gnome sees his opposite number and double appear and the story at last ends in death. The film is put back in its box, a small, coffin-shaped chest. The mythical cinema is always going back to the real life that stands behind the screen.

'In fact the audience takes on the image; it creates the film. The audience creates its own film,' Bringuier has said. We are led to wonder whether the cinema, however 'original' it may be, must not of necessity go back either to myth or to documentary as long as film alone, in relation to a fixed reality, introduces a revolutionary dimension.

The Research Team of the ORTF

In its June 1960 number, by one of those sly quirks of fate, *Cahiers du Cinéma* gave its readers two fundamental, unpublished texts which, looking back, embody the two trends I have pointed out in 'concrete cinema'. One was 'The Counterpoint of Sound and Image' by Pierre Schaeffer, the creator and director of the research team which had just been set up by French radio and television; the other was 'The New American Cinema' by Jonas Mekas, an article published in France before it appeared in the United States, which later became the charter of the American underground.

The introduction of *Cahiers du Cinéma* to Schaeffer's article said: 'The cinema was born silent. The image is the elder of the two. Direction comes first in the film, the dialogue only later, then music as an extra. Suppose this order were reversed? Suppose the musician and the poet prepared to get their own back? Suppose the progress of the cinema depended on a "drastic" revision of the relationship between sound and image?' Eric Rohmer, then chief editor of *Cahiers du Cinéma*, was writing this introduction anonymously, and thus foresaw the importance of what was to be done in the cinema by the old musical research group set up by Schaeffer in 1957, which became the research team of French radio and television in 1960 (today known as the ORTF). 'Between the nascent television and the already classic cinema relations have been wrongly established, links are poorly maintained,' wrote Pierre Schaeffer in the same year after a number of declarations, discussions and film-shows in June. '"New Wave" film-makers discovered what early film-makers had already tried out. The knowledge acquired by the cinema seems poorly used by television, and the questions concerned with television itself seem wrongly framed.' An attempt would be made to show 'common ground between disciplines as varied as those of the engineer, the artist, the economist and the sociologist'. It was a case of 'a disinterested study that went beyond the everyday'. And a serious note was, inevitably, struck: 'It is not a matter of pure research. Whether pure or impure – and the matter is debatable – it is a case of looking into professional probity, group

137

morality,' because 'if we are talking about aesthetics we must talk about ethics as well; if we are thinking of an elite then we must also think about the public in general; if we mention "the people" then we must know if we are using the word in a vulgar or a noble sense' (Pierre Schaeffer). A certain number of young experimental film-makers, the introduction to *Cahiers* said, 'tried to apply to their art the methods used with "musical objects" in what is known as "concrete music"'.

Schaeffer gave the tone to this remarkable study of the relations between sound and image in the cinema and summed up his idea of an art that was still in its infancy, trying, very modestly but very precisely, to reduce it to its elementary physical realities. At the beginning – and let us not forget that this was written in 1960, before the magnetic registration of images – he declared that one must make a true distinction between sound and image in the cinema. The real difference between them was that the image displayed itself in space, whereas sound displayed itself in time. The parallel was carefully maintained in the paragraphs and chapters that followed, Schaeffer seeing both sound and image as things that can be measured, referred to and coordinated very precisely. The image may be deployed in space but it also takes part – no less than sound does – in a temporal dimension with its own frequency, duration and rhythm. This means that there is a triple possibility of image and sound being related to each other; and a fourth and fundamental possibility also exists – that of synchronism. Carrying on the argument in a second chapter called 'Use of Objects', Pierre Schaeffer makes the obvious distinction, and immediately rejects it, between abstract and concrete, figurative and non-figurative, in both sound and vision; and he describes his own amazement at the shock his 'concrete' music produced, when 'abstract' cinema had been accepted for a very long time. Then he drew some conclusions about the possible relationships between the two languages – of music and cinema.

It is not so much the question of terminology that is interesting in this (the author, of course, calls 'abstract' our 'concrete' cinema); more important is Schaeffer's great interest in sound. This was, of course, quite natural in a man who has written *Traité des objets musicaux* in which he tries, for the
138

first time, to define all possible relationships between sound and image, from the simplest to the most complex. As research goes on, further relationships between sound and image will be sought equally naturally in the work of the major artists of our time, as well as raw synchronised documents.

The 'Underground', Myth and Reality

The 'underground' movement in the cinema, of which Jonas Mekas has set himself up as both pope and prophet, is still little known in many European countries. It represents a complete break with the idea of cinema as it has been handed down to us for generations by a great many artists. It is the only deliberate, coherent attempt to open up cinematic creation to everyone, to make it as individualised, as subjective, as concrete and as hand-made as the work of the painter, the sculptor or the composer. It is typically American and expresses the most radical reaction so far heard to the Hollywood system and the system of commercial cinema in general, even when it tries to look independent. Deeply anarchical, it denies that the cinema is a mass medium. A film, it says, is created for pleasure and answers to nothing but the individual whim. It falls into the category of concrete cinema twice over, first through its insistence on the fact that film-making is something exclusively personal, then in its use, either conscious or unconscious, of the old disciplines – poetry, painting, sculpture, and music.

In the article in *Cahiers du Cinéma* mentioned earlier, Jonas Mekas praises the French 'New Wave' and says that Jean Rouch's *Moi, un Noir* was a model for the 'new American cinema', although he preferred the first 16mm version of John Cassavetes' *Shadows* (later enlarged to 35mm with supplementary scenes added and a heavier rhythm): 'The language, the situations, the details of the action all have the freshness one associates with the word improvisation,' he writes. 'The episodes consisted of objectively improvised situations, events from which the spectator draws his own conclusions.' Later, Mekas analyses *Pull my Daisy*, by the photographer Robert Frank and the painter Alfred Leslie:

139

'A free improvision on a scene from an unperformed play by Jack Kerouac. We are shown an evening in Greenwich Village when a young man is visited by friends of his who are poets and who include the young "bishop" of some sect or other. The poets include the big names of the "Beat Generation" – Gregory Corso, Allen Ginsberg and Peter Orlowski, arguing, gesticulating, improvising as hard as they can . . . The film was made without sound. Jack Kerouac speaks for each person and discusses the action freely. While the commentary was being taken Kerouac improvised quite without preparation and knowing nothing about the film, in a sort of poetic trance, comparable to the visions of a drug addict. *Pull my Daisy* has no plot, follows no logical pattern. Above all, it is a portrait of the secret condition of a whole generation . . . insofar as "beat" is the expression of the younger generation's rejection, either conscious or unconscious, of middle-class and business attitudes. No pretensions, no lying, no moralising.'

Further on again, Jonas Mekas defines another major preoccupation of the 'new American cinema' in his unconditional praise of a film that Leacock also liked very much:

'This means mentioning another important preoccupation of the "new American cinema": the attempt to free the camera itself. This is what Stanley Brakhage has done perfectly in a short film called *Desistfilm*. In it he uses all the techniques of spontaneous cinema. He shows a young people's "wild party", their exhibitionism, their adolescent games, the whole thing filmed during a real improvised party, with a 16 mm camera, generally hand-held and savagely following the smallest movement without any prearranged plan . . . The continuous wave of life is caught, the film has the vitality, the rhythm and the temperament of a poem by Rimbaud, a harrowing, entirely improvised confession, in which one fails to notice the artist's hand, yet in which a certain distance is kept between reality and art.

'To sum up, it must now be clear that the new arts in America, among them the "new American cinema", are being born in a movement that is ethical rather than aesthetic. There

140

are more important things than aesthetics to build: there is the new man himself. Anyone who asks this generation for works of art with well-defined political and aesthetic positions should be locked up. We don't want that: we're still too young, too much alive. In the next ten years we shall see intensive research and further areas of feeling will be set free to penetrate the most secret, the least polluted corners of the human mind, in a desperate effort to escape the clichés of art and of life.

'The "new American cinema" has more confidence in intuition and improvision than in discipline. Like his colleagues, the dynamic painter, the poet or the dancer, the film-maker seeks to catch art in what is most fleeting and free: art as action, not as the *status quo*; art that expresses a continuum of feelings, not a series of facts, still-lifes or pastiches. And as the modern American film-maker wants, as Suzuki puts it, above all "to seize life from within and not from without", leaving things completely open to his own sensibility, his films might be called "spontaneous cinema".'

In September 1960 the New American Cinema Group was born, the object of its members being to help one another 'to produce their own films, find new channels to distribute them and, in general, go into all the practical aspects of their work' (Jonas Mekas, *New American Cinema*, published in June 1967 for the third New Cinema Festival at Pesaro). In 1962 the Film-Makers Cooperative was formed as well; this was open to all film-makers, time alone being the judge of their films' quality. The film itself gave them the right to join, the cooperative being – as it still is – run by the film-makers themselves. Everyone is free to withdraw his film at any time. A catalogue is sent out annually giving the details of each film, and what it costs to rent or even to buy it (the films are on sale from certain bookshops). The maker gets seventy five per cent of the gross profits. The films are sent to colleges, universities and art galleries. In 1966 the Film-makers Distribution Centre was set up to distribute the films in the commercial sector. The pioneers of 'experimental' American cinema (a name used before 'underground' came in, when only a handful of artists made films), who, in earlier days, might expect to make 300

141

dollars a year at the most – a sum that could hardly be expected to keep them going in the cinema – can today live moderately well and easily make between 6000 and 7000 dollars a year by having these same films distributed by the cooperative. Sometimes the cooperative lends a film-maker money. All the troubles have not yet been solved; some films never come out of the shadows, and the cooperative lacks the kind of structure that would allow it to grow into the enormous organisation it might easily become.

Despite its evident economic limitations, the 'new American cinema', as Mekas conceived it, made possible the creation of films in complete freedom and with very little money. Cutting rooms were set up, in which anyone could work on his own film whenever he wanted to. Cameras were collected and offered to young Negroes who wished to say how they saw America. In the best American tradition mystical ideas and a sense of reality achieved a remarkable degree of freedom in the cinema. There are now any number of groups, some of them socially more committed than Mekas, who have taken over his idea of absolute independence. And although there has been a good deal of wastage among the many people who today express themselves entirely spontaneously through the cinema, nonetheless, people who will never try to go to Hollywood have made their names as well; some of them narcissistic people jealously cultivating their own egos.

Today, one man dominates the 'new American cinema': Stan Brakhage, a lonely artist who rejects all compromise, a kind of underground mixture of Abel Gance and Antonioni who has gone as far as is possible and even beyond it in his renewal of the cinema as we know it – first by questioning it radically, finally by destroying it. In 'Metaphors on Vision', published in a special number of *Film Culture*, Brakhage declares his right to see everything, to look at everything:

'Imagine an eye that doesn't obey the rules of perspective as man has fashioned them, an eye free of all prejudice of compositional logic, an eye that doesn't answer to the name of each object but has to know whatever he meets in life through an adventure of perception. How many colours exist in a field covered in grass for the baby crawling over
142

it, unconscious of the word 'green'? How many rainbows can light create for the untamed eye? To what point can this eye be conscious of variations in waves of heat? Imagine a world full of incomprehensible objects glittering with an infinite variety of movements and gradations of colour. Imagine a world before "in the beginning was a word".'

So does Brakhage lay the foundations of an aesthetic outlook that may appear retrograde both in relation to what he himself managed to do in his first films, made with synchronised sound, and in relation to the whole of direct cinema, even in relation to what Pierre Schaeffer has been doing. The cinema becomes a substitute for the established arts, neurotically dominated and strangely linked with a number of fundamental obsessions. With his wife Jane, who has always been his colleague as well, Brakhage lives out the myth of the *artiste maudit* to its furthest limits. To him, the world of his films is more real than that of living beings and objects. *Anticipation of the Night* (1958) makes extraordinary play with colours and fleeting forms. *Window Water Baby Moving* (1959) is quite simply and directly both exalting and literally obscene: it shows us Jane in labour and the birth of their first child, a primitive, earthy poem with a strength that makes one reconsider the cinema entirely. In *Mothlight* (1966) dead butterflies were simply stuck on to the film. His most ambitious work, *The Art of Vision* (1961–65) takes the essential parts of an earlier four-part film, *Dog Star Man* with a prelude added to them, these four parts – A, B, C, D – being combined until the possibilities of the series are exhausted. But, Brakhage says, 'the form is conditioned by the works of art which inspired *Dog Star Man*, the growth of the form by the physiology and the experiences [including artistic experiences] of the man who made it'. *The Art of Vision* is a cosmic poem in which sunspots, the interior of the human body and family scenes are all mingled, and the audience is presupposed to have abandoned all critical reaction to the world around him. The very short 8mm *Songs* (1964, etc.) are even more striking, beautifully balanced between the plastic rigour of painting and the rhythmic quality of music. Song XIV, for instance, is described like this: 'A vision through closed eyes of moulds, paintings

143

LIVING CINEMA

and crystals.' Song XVI: 'A love song, sex flowering in the inner eye, joy.' For years Brakhage's films have been soundless – no noises, no words. Even when one has made all the usual reservations about the artist's lack of communication, Brakhage must be considered one of the greatest, the most complete artists of the old cinema – the cinema in which only the image counted, bastard child of all the established arts. We do not regret that, for a long period of time, Brakhage has stuck only to this 'bastard' approach, rejecting today's modern cinema born of the close and indestructible fusion of sight and sound, image and the living word. Uncompromising, he treads the lonely path of pure art.

The whole underground will be influenced by Brakhage's reckless approach. Certainly in the first place two well-known film-makers – Gregory Markopoulos, who made *Twice a Man* (1963), which won the *grand prix* at the festival of experimental films at Knokke-le-Zoute in 1964 (its rhythm was at times very fast, one new image each frame, that is 24 different images a second); and the more classical Kenneth Anger, who accompanies his narrative with overwhelming music, either classical or pop (*Scorpio Rising*, 1964). But Brakhage, Markopoulos and Anger are, all things being equal, rather what you might call the Gance, Clément and Vadim of the 'underground'. Among the others Michael Snow, a painter who won the *grand prix* at the festival of experimental films at Knokke-le-Zoute in 1967, must be mentioned. Of his prize-winning film he said when presenting it:

'*Wavelength* was filmed in a week, preceded by a year of notes, thoughts, and wondering. I wanted to make a résumé of my nervous system, my religious inclinations and my aesthetic ideas. I wanted to conceive a temporal monument in which the beauty and the sadness of equivalence would be celebrated, I wanted to try to make a definitive declaration of a purely filmic space and time, a balance of 'illusion' and 'reality', all turning on vision. Space begins at the level of the camera's eye (the audience's eye), is in the air, then on the screen, then in the screen (the spirit) . . . The film is a continual zoom which takes forty-five minutes from its

144

largest to its smallest, and final, take. It was filmed with a camera fixed at the end of an attic twenty-four yards long, with a row of windows and the street at the other end. Thus, the décor and the action which appear in it are cosmic equivalents. The room (and the zoom) are interrupted by four human events, including a death. The sound on these occasions is synchronised, music and words being heard simultaneously with electronic music, a sinusoidal wave that moves from its lowest level (50 cycles a second) to its highest (12,000 cycles a second) in forty minutes. It is a total glissando, while the film is a crescendo, a dispersed spectrum that seeks to use the gifts of prophecy and memory, the only things the film and music have to offer.'

This strange preoccupation with both physics and metaphysics closely interwoven became even more evident and all-pervading in the unique *La Région centrale* (1971), shot on a peak in Quebec with a specially built camera, able to move horizontally, vertically and laterally, but always in continuous circles. Curiously enough here concrete cinema, as we have tried to define it, gets closer and closer to direct cinema, but throws us into a world before the word, before civilisation, before (or after) the history of man. By the sheer nature of this circular, uninterrupted movement, counterpointed by a purely electronic sound synchronised with the image, the process of human thinking and creativity seems to be offered to us in all its purity and nakedness.

Conclusion

We are entering the age of the relative, in which individual choice may play an increasingly large part, but in a completely different perspective from that of past centuries. Besides, we are entering into an age of mass manipulation where contradiction will be needed more than ever. Television and the cinema, henceforward inseparable, even though the nature of the new medium born of their meeting had never been properly defined, urge us to explore all the dimensions of our universe, at once so vast and so infinitesimally small. New techniques are multiplied and all-powerful mathematics allow us to see the possibility of pushing the frontiers of knowledge further and further. And, at the very moment in which man can seriously envisage the conquest of the cosmos, or at least a part of it, a cosmos that is gigantic only in the perspective of Pascal's 'two infinites', we may wonder what these new techniques may bring with them; techniques, or rather proceedings, studied didactically in these pages, with all their mythical and effective potential, which create new illusions, the dangerous effects of which should be countered.

First of all Richard Leacock's primary position and importance were stressed. There is no 'cult of personality' in this; merely the fact that by making a man who is closely in contact with the machine our mediator, breathing through his machine in a way, we establish a new relationship with our own small world.

'When a film claims to be real, I get angry!' Leacock used to say at the beginning of his partnership with Robert Drew. In the same way he denounced the fake-theatre that passed as theatre: 'In the old days the actor wore a mask, he didn't claim to be performing realistically.' Marshall McLuhan, by emphasising the varying degrees of participation offered by television, with which each person is at once free and participating intensely, is brought to the same idea as Leacock and to Brecht's essential preoccupation: knowing and touching what is concrete on condition that one is not lost in it. That is what Pierre Schaeffer expressed at the round table conference on the mass media organised by Unesco in August 1968 in Montreal, as well as in an educational broadcast of the National Film Board of Canada called *Image, que veux-tu?* directed by André Martin: 'The tool of participation,' said Schaeffer, 'tends to become a tool of non-participation . . . Shall we have "efficacious participators" or "paralysed spectators"? The hand must not allow itself to become insensitive.' Quite rightly he tempered the enthusiasm of some who had recently taken up electronics by warning them to bear in mind what is called the 'Third World', a world that is rising a little in all kinds of places yet in present-day conditions will not achieve the Western and, in particular, the American way of life for a very long time. In the same broadcast Pierre Schaeffer wondered if there was not a 'failure of art': 'He [man] is trying to escape into a cult of things, sounds, images, which hides his profound panic . . . We are surrounded by sound and images. It is time to give back a meaning to it all.'

Direct cinema is one answer, first of all. This means direct cinema not merely as television 'made directly', but the result of work that is often harder and more radical than any in the old cinema, even when it is dressed in the tinsel trappings of modernity. Personalities do not much matter; what matters is to catch the revolutionary character of what these men have done, and at least to understand that on the level of pure cinema – to use a stupid term – they are living through an adventure many times more exciting than that of the early pioneers who created the great Hollywood early in the century with a few pieces of wood and string. This kind of cinema may be less spectacular, and above all it needs other conditions of projection and participation. The barrier of language can always be overcome by simultaneous translation, which demands an effort on the part of those concerned with it as great, or rather of the same kind, as that of the film-maker himself. They too must move from the written to the spoken word, from what is told to what is lived. This cinema, which is not cinema in the old sense, or television either, demands thought, a perpetual exchange with the screen, and self-criticism even on the part of the audience. It cannot be reduced to the kind of performance we know at present.

Concrete cinema is the other end of the pole. Here, too, the artist of the scientific century is seeking to give new insights, new feelings and new experiences to the audience, snug in its own comfortable *ideés reçues*. Like direct cinema in the widest sense it is ceaselessly one of sight and hearing, the two senses through which, for lack of anything better, we establish our relationships with others. Both of them may allow amateurism but, as the work of Richard Leacock and Norman McLaren shows, they demand a very high technical level and a sharp awareness of all the possibilities of the tools employed. In the near future those who have mastered the use of these tools must be put in touch at last with those who have nothing at all. It is a scandal that the 'new cinema', while it is often misunderstood in the so-called civilised countries, is not accessible to the new countries because they are poor. Perhaps we are not ready to give them the chance of making a clean sweep of all our outdated models.

'The cinema will tell the world about unity,' wrote the French critic Léon Moussinac, in the silent film era. Never has it been so imperative, never has the opportunity been greater, to discover new continents on this earth of ours.

Postscript: Into the Seventies

Since 1968 direct cinema – that is, films in which language is all-important – has found growing support among those who favour realism in the raw, but has not managed to find the same support among the admirers of classical cinema, with its predominantly visual heritage from the silent films. Jean-Luc Godard has worsened the situation by denouncing the pseudo-realism of light film with synchronised sound as the most advanced example of cinematic illusion. For, he says, the cinema in no way reflects reality, it is merely the reality of a reflection. To the latest puritans of film criticism – those writing for the new-style *Cahiers du Cinéma* and for *Cinéthique* which appeared after 1968, both of them wedded to a pure, hard-line Marxism-Leninism – if the director's whim is no more than an article of faith, direct cinema *is* the cinema's original sin. It's no surprise that two film-makers who were always interested in the problem of direct cinema using synchronised sound, Jean-Marie Straub, French-born but for a time working in Germany, and Jean-Luc Godard who is French by adoption, have been promoted to the role of avant-garde directors for having revealed, once and for all, the cinema's way of tricking both eye and ear.

The most paradoxical and in my view the most aggressive attitude is Straub's: somehow using direct cinema with synchronised sound to emasculate the spoken word. For instance he has adapted a German novel by Heinrich Böll in *Nicht versöhnt (Unreconciled)*, and filmed in its entirety a play of Corneille, written when he was old, *Othon*. In both cases the actors are either wholly non-professional or not really influenced by the ties of their profession. The director sets off a curious process in which speech as such disintegrates; and he uses a strong stylised diction with no attempt at realism, or rather at naturalism. The important parts of *Nicht versöhnt* are those in which the characters either declaim long tirades without the smallest appearance of verisimilitude, or else repeat parts of sentences again and again. The process is even more obvious in *Othon*. The director makes his actors 'recite' Corneille, rather as if they were at school, with extreme precision and thoroughness (but no care for the rules of correct speech or the methods of the Comédie Française!): each man is free to be himself, to confront the text alone, in his own way. This makes both actors and audience feel uneasy, and a different kind of truth steals into what is happening, and words take on a new dimension. Perhaps Jean-Marie Straub is trying, unconsciously, to remind us that when our civilisation began there were two strictly distinct kinds of language, the written and the spoken, and that written language, although rich in all the ambiguities of the spoken word, must always remain the basic source of our ideas and thinking.

In 1968 Jean-Luc Godard, using recent events as a base, made a 'militant' film called *Un Film comme les Autres*, in 16mm colour and with synchronised sound. Students and young workers who had taken part in the uprisings of May 1968 discuss their actions and put forward their views, while newsreel pictures occasionally illustrate or counterpoint what they are saying. Godard's camera, in a way not unlike Straub's, makes the audience feel uneasy, at a distance from the group, which continues to argue endlessly in a back yard near a factory. We see the group, but without knowing who says what. The words spoken fall as relentlessly as blows from an axe and take on a new dimension: the audience is obliged to think, rather than lulled into merely identifying one or other young militant's face with what is being said. In 1972 Godard returned to the commercial cinema, that is to the kind of film that would be shown on the general circuits, after a long time making films for a more restricted audience. With his new collaborator Jean-Pierre Gorin, he made a quite remarkable film, with Yves Montand and Jane Fonda in it, aimed at the general public and called *Tout va bien*. In it, Godard sticks more closely than ever to his belief that the audience must not identify with the characters on the screen. In the first part, which is – to use the old Soviet term – very 'agit-prop', Godard and Gorin show the many aspects of a strike in which the boss

150

is held by the strikers in a hilarious, Mayakovsky-type style. The second, much stronger, part of the film shows the relationship of the couple affected by these events. He is a progressive film-maker of impeccable left-wing views, she an American journalist who is waking up to political and economic reality. Elia Kazan and Arthur Penn have shown us scenes in which couples behave even more violently than in these; but Godard goes much further, and seems to be carrying on from where he left off before 1968. He strips the actor, and probes him personally, as well as the character he is playing. Yves Montand and Jane Fonda's faces, and the tone of their voices, show that a double development is taking place, working from the character to the actor and vice versa. Perhaps this is only a single case in which direct cinema really breaks through, and the proof Richard Leacock keeps asking for so insistently that language itself becomes an essential part of the action.

The problem of pure direct cinema is not so easily solved; that is, a cinema in which no liberating fiction is involved and there is no question of the credibility of what is shown. A recent film shows the danger of a certain form of direct cinema – let us call it 'reportage' – when it fails to be critical enough of its premises. This is Marcel Ophuls' *The Sorrow and the Pity* (*Le Chagrin et la Pitié*), now already regarded as a classic. The film's huge success, with both French audiences and English-speaking ones, is first of all due to the fact that it deals with a period of French history about which very little is known, a period shrouded in legend – the years of the German Occupation and of the Liberation that came after it. In one famous sequence, that of the interview with Christian de la Mazière, who was once in the Waffen ss, de la Mazière explains how it was natural for him, as a member of the upper middle class, the traditional defender of national values, to find himself fighting on the side of the Germans on the eastern front, in the name of those same values. André Harris, Marcel Ophuls' collaborator in the making of the film, who had worked particularly in television, conducted the interview; what he turned out was extremely effective but totally uncritical: never once did he challenge the arguments put forward by the man he was interviewing. This proves the dangers of direct cinema, so much feared by the young French 'Marxist-Leninist'

151

critics. A part of the truth appears to be the whole truth, with all the emotive power of which direct cinema is capable.

From West Germany comes another film using political analysis in a much subtler way and with much greater control, *Der Hamburger Aufstand: Oktober 1923* (*The Rising in Hamburg in October 1923*). Its makers are Klaus Wildenhahn, who teaches at the Deutsche Film Akademie in West Berlin, and two of his pupils, Reiner Etz and Gisela Tuchtenhagen. They discovered the survivors of the only Communist uprising ever to take place in Germany, in October 1923, when the German working class was strongly influenced by what was taking place in the Soviet Union, although the Nazi movement was also starting up at the same time. The survivors, who in 1923 were young militants in the Communist Party, are made to speak; while writings from the period, and places filled with historical associations, counterpoint what they are saying about an event that has been completely expunged from official history books. By the use of unusually discreet montage the film contrasts past and present, the fat faces of contemporary Germans of 1971, and their far from innocent ideas grown out of their revolutionary experience. Made for the absurd sum of 15,000 marks, a film like this was possible only as a result of very careful advance preparations: by getting progressively familiar with atmosphere and people long before shooting took place the film-makers became 'accepted' by those who were asked to speak in it. Unlike the films of Jean-Marie Straub, in which economy of expression leads to the wish to cut out language altogether, this film shows that it is language alone that makes the performance exist, that shapes the image, and that demands from the audience a degree of participation which few are prepared to give.

But it is in Canada, and mainly in French-speaking Canada, that direct cinema, quite apart from the centrally important work of Pierre Perrault, has found an ideal outlet. In his remarkable *Québec: Duplessis et après* (1972), Denys Arcand filmed the 1971 provincial elections in Quebec, and followed the main political parties. He based his action upon two texts which come up again and again: one was the Durham Report of 1834, describing the very low material and intellectual level of French Canadians, the other the 'catechism' of the National

152

Union Party in 1936, analysing the possibilities of social change in French-Canadian society. Rather as happened in Klaus Wildenhahn's film, past and present illumine each other. But in this it is the past that is the catalyst. In a French-speaking country like Quebec, where the language has to stand up for its autonomy in the face of the traditional linguistic imperialism of the French spoken in France, the cinema of language, or direct cinema, has naturally played a leading role in the development of political awareness which has taken place on the banks of the St Lawrence over the past few years. Apart from the films of Pierre Perrault and Denys Arcand there is Arthur Lamothe's *Le Mépris n'aura qu'un Temps,* on the condition of building workers in Montreal, and Fernand Dansereau's *Faut aller parmi le Monde pour le savoir*, a militant film addressed to the common people of Quebec. Unlike those of Perrault and Arcand, which were subsidised by the National Film Board, these films were made very cheaply. Lamothe's was financed and then distributed by the trade unions, Dansereau's, which is divided into three parts, is called 'kitchen-cinema' by its maker; that is, it will be shown in kitchens, to families, with a qualified person there to give any explanations that may be needed.

Obviously it is in the United States that direct cinema has been developed furthest. Private enterprise misses no opportunity of bearing witness to this or that cause, or of dealing with this or that subject, although the teachings of Richard Leacock, whom inevitably one must refer to, are not always properly assimilated. Two recent examples show the degree of skill already achieved by his heirs, although this is not necessarily a case of cause and effect. On the one hand, a group of young film-makers at the beginning of 1971 shot, in Detroit, the hearings of 'Veterans against the Vietnam war', and, after twelve months' cutting, turned it into the film *Winter Soldier*. The direction, where deliberately no name is mentioned, merely shows in a very carefully calculated progression a series of overwhelming statements made by veterans of the Vietnam war, aged between twenty and twenty-seven. Audience and participants, behind and in front of the camera, at times understand simultaneously the appalling drama that took place. On the other hand there is Emile de Antonio's *Milhouse* (1972), a

153

satire on President Nixon which its maker has called 'a white comedy'. This never bothers with realism for a moment but, with a masterly use of montage that rediscovers some of the virtues of classical montage, manages to juxtapose contradictory elements which produce a third kind of reality. De Antonio shows us a character who is continually acting, cultivating his own brand image and at the same time showing unbridled ambition in every moment. Richard Milhouse Nixon, seen by de Antonio, seems to have escaped from a Frank Capra comedy edited with the unfailing sense of humour of a Leo McCarey; playing the American success game for all it is worth, he appears the complete all-American boy. The audience must be ready to accept – indeed to 'read' – the director's message; it must face its own prejudices with these fragments of living reality, put together in such a way that word cuts in upon words, as with the films of Pierre Perrault, rather than image upon image, as in classical montage.

One p.m., by D. A. Pennebaker, Richard Leacock's faithful collaborator and maker of *Don't Look Back*, is his montage of the material filmed by himself and Leacock of Jean-Luc Godard's visit to New York in 1968. Godard was dissatisfied with the work of his cameramen and so refused to go ahead with the film. *One p.m.* is unique of its kind and should be analysed in detail. In it, involuntarily, Godard's technique, which recreates direct cinema entirely through a particular sensibility, and Leacock's technique, which gives absolute priority to the untouched event and to those taking part in it, confront each other in an exemplary way. Leacock and Pennebaker, holding the camera turn and turn about and sometimes filming together, unknown to him, film Godard directing. Godard makes reality burst out from the way he directs, and from the way he places and arranges what is filmed; Leacock, on the contrary, seeks to match the original rhythm of the event, the very way in which a character breathes – in a way, he works outwards from the inside. To see this film once is not enough; it may not truly satisfy anyone but it is very revealing about the technical and human implications of both direct cinema as Leacock conceived it and '*cinéma d'auteur*' as the French 'New Wave' defined it.

Jean Rouch's short film *Turu* (1972) shows the influence of

154

both Perrault and Leacock in a limited way. The 16mm synchronised camera is held at arm's length and analyses a very clearly defined phenomenon – in this case, two people beating a drum and becoming possessed – breaking down this phenomenon through a previous knowledge of the subject. Then there is the extra touch Jean Rouch loves, which means that the camera does not merely register what is happening objectively but takes part in it and modifies it. In this vignette Jean Rouch knows how the dance is going to develop before he breaks it down with the camera, for he has already broken it down in his head; but his insistent presence makes the dancers go on and on. In spite of all the reservations Leacock and Perrault might have – for very different reasons – about his progress, Rouch shows that an intangible, unchangeable reality, one that has existed for all eternity, simply does not make sense. Perhaps, starting from there, the task of direct cinema is to show perpetually moving reality through the very movement of the spoken word, through which man affirms his presence in the world.

Perhaps direct cinema means the cinema of the spoken word. It implies a new perception of reality, starting from which we shall have to reconstruct the entire cinema and invent a new dramaturgy. Perhaps what we have been living through is merely the cinema's prehistory.

On the other hand, cinema, in its classical sense which is basically visual, may have reached an all-time perfection with *La Région centrale*. Concrete cinema, as the ultimate accomplishment of the visual arts, points to the disappearance of all our worn-out mental schemes, suggests the emergence of a new man, using words but also brand-new concepts. A new cinema shall bear witness to this.

5.16.96, GIFT, 63813
(3.95)